Storm Over Europe

Storm Over Europe

Allied Bombing Missions in the Second World War

JUAN VÁZQUEZ GARCÍA

Translated by
Steve Turpin White

Pen & Sword
MILITARY

AN IMPRINT OF PEN & SWORD BOOKS LTD.
YORKSHIRE - PHILADELPHIA

First published in 2017 by Galland Books as *Los diablos de la noche* and *Tormenta sobre Europa*

First published in Great Britain in 2019 by
Pen & Sword Military
An imprint of
Pen & Sword Books Ltd
Yorkshire - Philadelphia

ISBN 978 1 52674 098 4

Typeset by Aura Technology and Software Services, India
Printed and bound in India
By Replika Press Pvt. Ltd.

Pen & Sword Books Ltd incorporates the Imprints of Pen & Sword Books Archaeology, Atlas, Aviation, Battleground, Discovery, Family History, History, Maritime, Military, Naval, Politics, Railways, Select, Transport, True Crime, Fiction, Frontline Books, Leo Cooper, Praetorian Press, Seaforth Publishing, Wharncliffe and White Owl.

For a complete list of Pen & Sword titles please contact

PEN & SWORD BOOKS LIMITED
47 Church Street, Barnsley, South Yorkshire, S70 2AS, England
E-mail: enquiries@pen-and-sword.co.uk
Website: www.pen-and-sword.co.uk

or

PEN AND SWORD BOOKS
1950 Lawrence Rd, Havertown, PA 19083, USA
E-mail: uspen-and-sword@casematepublishers.com
Website: www.penandswordbooks.com

Contents

PART ONE

Night Devils: British Bomber Command

1

The Origins of Bomber Command

The first strategic bombings in history date back to early in the First World War, when the *British Royal Naval Air Service* attacked *Zeppelin* bases at Cologne and Düsseldorf towards the end of 1914, to which the Germans responded by attacking Dover and Erith. But these operations were on a very small scale indeed, limited by the resources available at the time.

The raids made by *Zeppelins* and, in particular, the German heavy bombers *Gotha* and *Giant* over British territory were a foretaste of what strategic bombing would be like in the next war. Given the limited effectiveness of existing defences against this threat, it was believed that the only effective response was to fight fire with fire. And so what was needed was a specialized and independent structure, which in time led to the creation of the *Royal Air Force* in April 1918 and, in June of the same year, of the *Independent Air Force*, the first unit set up specifically for strategic bombing.

The first aircraft with strategic capacity was the *Handley Page 0/400*, capable of carrying 1,500 kg of bombs. The new doctrine already had many staunch supporters, Trenchard, who would be head of the Air Staff for ten years, being one of them. Convinced that the only effective response was counter-attack, he claimed that the effect on morale of the bombings was greater than the purely physical effect. According to him the only aircraft capable of winning a war were heavy bombers and fighters were no more than mere elements of propaganda. For Trenchard, true air superiority consisted of being able to carry a larger bomb payload further than the enemy.

1. Trenchard's theories would remain valid for decades. But he was short-sighted when it came to identifying and addressing the air force's shortcomings in the 1930s. A large proportion of the budget was spent on extravagant clubs and quarters for officers rather than on aircraft.

2. One of the first strategic bombers, a 1916 German Gotha.

During the twenties and thirties there was a constant stream of studies and debates on the true potential of strategic bombing, with each country reaching its own conclusions. Germany, after the experience of tactical bombing during the Spanish Civil War, decided to forgo the development of a truly strategic bomber in favour of optimizing their medium bombers. The United Kingdom fell somewhat behind in terms of weapons technology with the result that in the early 1930s its air force could only be described as mediocre in the extreme.

In 1932, Prime Minister Baldwin declared that, since bombers would be unstoppable, the only possible response was counter-attack, for which a special unit would have to be developed. It would be another four years before Bomber Command was set up, with very limited resources. A simulation conducted during the 1938 Munich crisis showed that neither the number nor the quality of the British bombers was sufficient to constitute an effective force.

But the philosophy behind the creation of Bomber Command, under a single independent command and with the sole purpose of attacking strategic targets, was clearly different from German thinking at the time. It was to be an offensive force whose mission would be to identify targets, develop the technology required to destroy them, and train aircrews to carry out that mission. Among the first targets identified were communications hubs in Germany, synthetic fuel production facilities, and the many industrial plants in the Ruhr Valley.

FIRST STRATEGIC BOMBERS

The first aircraft used by the British to attack strategic targets was the *De Havilland DH-9*, a light bomber capable of carrying bombs of up to 250 kg, which proved to be of very limited value.

The first truly strategic bomber was the *Handley Page 0/400*, capable of carrying up to 1,650 kg of bombs with a range of over one thousand kilometres. It was followed by the *Vickers Vimy*, able to reach Berlin with a 1,200 kg bomb payload, but they were completed too late to play any part in the war. The *Vickers Virginia* was the standard heavy bomber of the RAF between 1924 and 1937. In this period the aircraft was constantly developed until the final version could carry nearly 1,500 kg of bombs with a range of 1,600 km. It had a top speed of 175 km/h and a service ceiling of 4,800 m. Despite its long service life it was not so different from the 1917 *Vimy*.

The Vickers Virginia was the main British bomber with strategic capacity for over a decade.

By 1936, long-range four-engine aircraft had been commissioned but their development and delivery were suffering from significant delays. Also, coincident with the war in Spain, there was a certain degree of political pressure calling for priority to be given to Fighter Command, resulting in the appearance of the *Hurricane* and, especially, the excellent *Spitfire*. These fighters, used as interceptors, would spearhead Britain's air defence, which in 1939, thanks to the development of radar, was one of the most advanced in the world.

However, the Air Staff continued to study plans for strategic offensives, known as Western Air Plans, with the aim of attacking Germany's synthetic oil industry, its hydroelectric plants and its transport network, while undermining the morale of the German population.

Strangely, these plans failed to take into sufficient account the problems posed by the technical limitations on navigation, target identification, or, of course, the ability to hit any targets with a minimum degree of accuracy. Neither did they consider the effectiveness of the new generation of fighters against bombers, even though the British air force had already developed the *Spitfire*. Throughout the war the strategists clung to a belief in the self-defensive capacity of close formations in daytime operations and in the ability to avoid enemy fighters and return home on night raids.

The Ruhr was the principal target of the British long-range bombing strategists during the 1930s.

PORTAL

Charles Portal flew on combat missions during the Great War and was one of the first airmen to bomb German territory. During the 1930s he was one of the architects of the expansion of the RAF and in April 1940 he became head of Bomber Command.

Highly appreciated by his colleagues, Portal had a reputation for being straightforward and honest. Very shy, he liked to dine alone at his London club every day. A staunch defender of strategic bombing, he continued to support it and the men who carried it out when he was appointed Chief of Air Staff in October 1940, a position he held until the end of the war.

The start of the war appeared to prove the pre-war theorists right, especially after the invasion of Poland and the period known as the Phoney War in which there were scarcely any operations and it seemed as if there would be plenty of time to make thorough preparations for any future conflict.

Despite the appeals and declarations of the first weeks of the conflict calling for the civilian population to be respected, soon both sides began to blur the boundaries between military and civilian targets. However, Bomber Command was initially limited by political and legal constraints, reflecting the British idea that indiscriminate bombing was a sign of barbarity while targeted bombing was a sign of civilization. But, over and above any ideological reasons, at the start of the war there were serious reasons of a more material nature for not engaging in a campaign of indiscriminate bombing. First and foremost among those reasons was a lack of the required equipment.

In September 1939 Bomber Command had 33 squadrons and nearly 500 aircraft of all types, divided into five groups spread over the south of England. Ten were equipped with the *Fairey Battle*, a light tactical bomber which would be shot out of the sky in the first days of the western campaign. Another six squadrons had

The effects of an on-target raid.

TWIN-ENGINE BOMBERS

During the three first years of the war most Bomber Command operations were carried out by twin-engine bombers poorly suited to the missions they were entrusted with.

ARMSTRONG WHITWORTH WHITLEY

When this aircraft entered service in 1937 it was a considerable improvement on what went before but its limitations would soon become apparent. It was used in numerous propaganda leaflet drops and was the first aircraft to drop bombs on German territory.

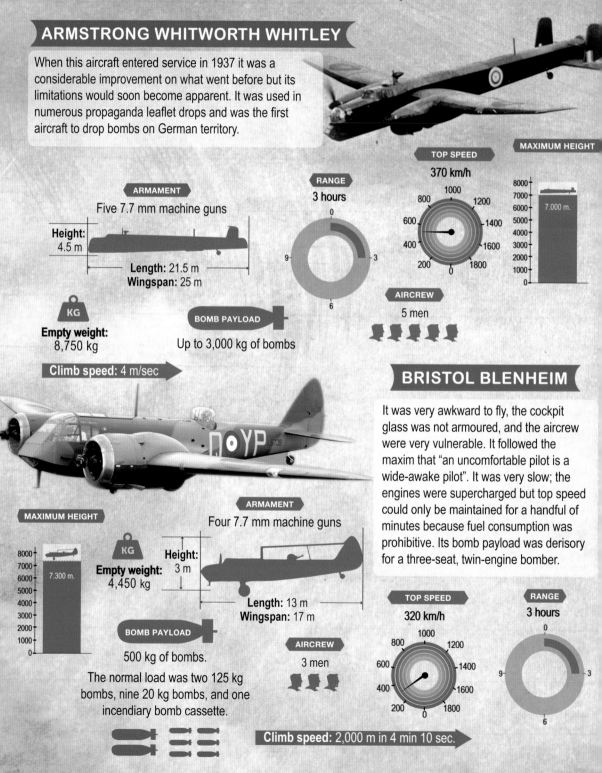

MAXIMUM HEIGHT
7.000 m.

TOP SPEED
370 km/h

RANGE
3 hours

ARMAMENT
Five 7.7 mm machine guns

Height: 4.5 m

Length: 21.5 m
Wingspan: 25 m

KG
Empty weight: 8,750 kg

BOMB PAYLOAD
Up to 3,000 kg of bombs

AIRCREW
5 men

Climb speed: 4 m/sec

BRISTOL BLENHEIM

It was very awkward to fly, the cockpit glass was not armoured, and the aircrew were very vulnerable. It followed the maxim that "an uncomfortable pilot is a wide-awake pilot". It was very slow; the engines were supercharged but top speed could only be maintained for a handful of minutes because fuel consumption was prohibitive. Its bomb payload was derisory for a three-seat, twin-engine bomber.

MAXIMUM HEIGHT
7.300 m.

KG
Empty weight: 4,450 kg

Height: 3 m

ARMAMENT
Four 7.7 mm machine guns

Length: 13 m
Wingspan: 17 m

BOMB PAYLOAD
500 kg of bombs.
The normal load was two 125 kg bombs, nine 20 kg bombs, and one incendiary bomb cassette.

AIRCREW
3 men

TOP SPEED
320 km/h

RANGE
3 hours

Climb speed: 2,000 m in 4 min 10 sec.

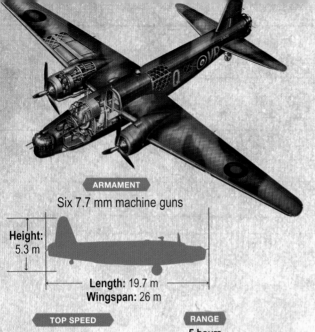

VICKERS WELLINGTON

The Wellington was built using a Barnes Wallis designed geodetic airframe which gave it great structural strength. It entered service in 1938 and became Bomber Command's main bomber until well into 1942, representing a huge qualitative leap compared to previous aircraft.

Very sturdy, fitted with modern hydraulically operated turrets, its most serious defect was its lack of self-sealing fuel tanks, which made it very vulnerable. In a variety of versions it remained in service until the end of the war.

ARMAMENT
Six 7.7 mm machine guns

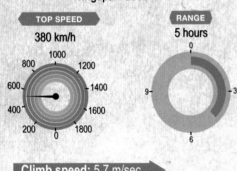

Height: 5.3 m
Length: 19.7 m
Wingspan: 26 m

TOP SPEED
380 km/h

RANGE
5 hours

MAXIMUM HEIGHT
5.500 m.

KG
Empty weight: 8,450 kg

BOMB PAYLOAD
Up to 2,000 kg of bombs

AIRCREW
6 men

Climb speed: 5.7 m/sec

HANDLEY PAGE HAMPDEN

The Hampden entered into service in the summer of 1938 and was soon highly appreciated by its aircrews, due to its speed and manoeuvrability. Airmen called it the "Flying Suitcase" due to the cramped conditions imposed by the narrowness of its fuselage.

The Hampden was crewed by five men: pilot, co-pilot, navigator, radio-operator, and machine gunner. When its days as a bomber were over it was used as a long-range torpedo bomber with only modest success.

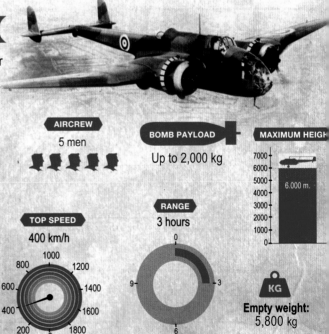

AIRCREW
5 men

BOMB PAYLOAD
Up to 2,000 kg

MAXIMUM HEIGH
6.000 m.

TOP SPEED
400 km/h

RANGE
3 hours

KG
Empty weight: 5,800 kg

ARMAMENT
Five 7.7 mm machine guns

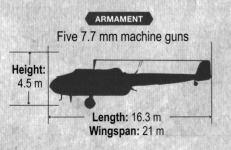

Height: 4.5 m
Length: 16.3 m
Wingspan: 21 m

Climb speed: 5 m/sec

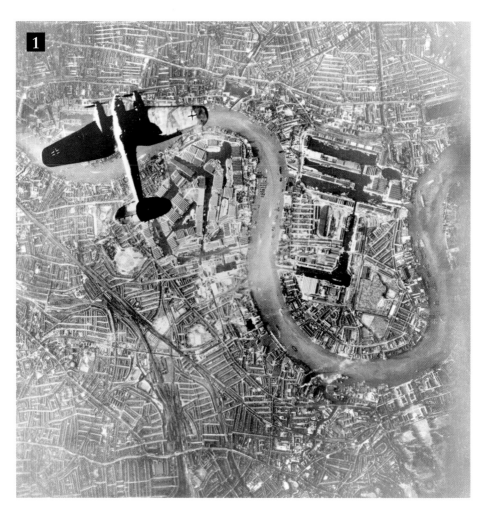

1. A German He 111 over London in 1940.

2. A London street hit by Luftwaffe bombs during the Blitz.

3. RAF commanders were convinced that the Wellington could defend itself effectively against German fighters thanks to its modern hydraulic turrets.

the twin-engine *Blenheim IV*, also a tactical bomber. The rest flew twin-engine *Hampden*, *Whitley* and *Wellington* bombers, all poorly suited to a strategic offensive. Many long months would have to pass before the first four-engine bombers entered service. Only the *Wellington* was capable of carrying out missions of any importance; they would still be making up half the bombing force in 1942 and various versions would remain in service until the end of the war.

The aircrews were inexperienced, the ground facilities were not suitable for large-scale operations, there was no way of identifying targets or reaching them with a sufficient number of aircraft, and the United States had refused to sell Britain any *Norden* bombsights which meant that bombing accuracy left much to be desired.

Navigators continued to use the stars to plot course and position, and electronic navigation aids were non-existent. The explosive power of the bombs used was limited (half that of equivalent German bombs of the same weight) and the two kilo magnesium incendiary bombs were too small (although they would continue to be used throughout the war). Accuracy was negligible. The primitive Mk 7 bombsight required a perfectly stable target approach for the last few kilometres for the drop to be marginally accurate.

The first combat experiences were far from promising. Initially limited to military targets on the German coast (Heligoland, Sylt and Wilhelmshaven), a small raid on 4 September suffered 23 per cent losses while from another, larger one on the 29th, half the *Hampdens* failed to return. After this bloodbath, operations were limited to night time, a solution which British theorists had already believed was the safest method.

But during the following months most of the bombers' missions would be restricted to leaflet drops over German cities, operations which were not only pointless but also costly, due to the high accident rate during the night flights. The aircrews' morale began to suffer seriously and operational capacity declined to such an extent that in April 1940 (shortly before the German offensive on the Western Front), Portal, the new head of Bomber Command, estimated that his 260 serviceable aircraft would only be capable of flying 36 missions a day after two weeks of actual combat.

During the first two years of the war the pilots of each aircraft had a great deal of freedom to carry out missions according to their own criteria.

On 10 May, the same day as the German attack on France and the Low Countries, Chamberlain's government, which had opposed attacks on German cities, was replaced by Churchill's, which had far fewer qualms about bombing civilian targets and was in favour of an unrestricted air offensive. On the following night thirty-seven British light and medium bombers attacked the German city of München Gladbach, killing four civilians (including a British woman who happened to be living there).

On 15 May the War Cabinet approved the development of a strategy to unleash a bombing offensive against any target that might have military connotations, without taking into consideration the likelihood of civilian victims. That same night a hundred or so bombers attacked various targets in the Ruhr Valley. The swift collapse of the French Front meant that tactical support missions were prohibited and all available bombers were reserved for missions against industrial targets.

The start of Bomber Command's air offensive against an increasingly broad range of targets, until indiscriminate bombing against German cities became the order of the day, was the result of a number of different factors. A government, presided over by Churchill, anxious to punish the alleged evil of the German people, past, present or future, together with pressure from RAF commanders (since the start of the war) to let them demonstrate what strategic bombing was capable of achieving, became a devastating combination.

Many theorists were convinced that the Ruhr was the German Achilles' heel and that an unrestricted air offensive in that vital region could bring Germany to its

The Hampden would enjoy a second career flying anti-shipping missions, armed with torpedoes.

knees in just a few weeks. One very optimistic study reached the conclusion that 4,000 sorties would be needed, based on the supposition that eight bomb impacts could destroy a power plant and twelve an aqueduct. This fantasy assumed a low-level bombing bomb error of less than 70 metres, while for medium level bombing the figure was estimated to be 270 metres. None of this had been tested under real combat conditions and reality soon showed how absurd those estimates were.

GUIDELINES

The rules of the game had changed. The August 1939 guidelines, which considered attacks causing victims among the civil population to be unlawful, were scrapped on 4 June 1940. Although the intentional killing of civilians continued to be considered a violation of international law, such deaths were acceptable if they were "*proportional*" when "*targets of military value in a broad sense*" (factories, refineries, communication nodes, etc.) were being attacked. A month later restrictions were relaxed even more until in October, after the German bombing of London, all restrictions were lifted.

On 30 October guidelines received by Bomber Command were based on concentrating on undermining the morale of the enemy through the systematic destruction of their major cities to show the German people what bombing is capable of doing.

2

The First Strategic Offensives

In the summer of 1940 the capacity of British bombers to cause significant damage to German industry was minimal. It was very difficult to locate the target, let alone hit it with bombs and, even when the target was hit, the damage inflicted was negligible. The number of aircraft attacking a specific target was very low, often between twenty and thirty, under the naïve assumption that a few bomb hits could destroy a factory. The results were disheartening. Aircraft often failed to even find the city where the target was cited, despite the best efforts of the aircrews. Between June and August nearly 8,700 missions were flown but very little was achieved, except for causing the Germans to strengthen their anti-aircraft defences.

> **CHURCHILL TO LORD BEAVERBROOK**
>
> **Minister of Aircraft Production, 8 July 1940**
>
> *"…there is one thing that will bring him back and bring him down, and that is an absolutely devastating, exterminating attack by very heavy bombers from this country upon the Nazi homeland."*

In September 1940 the order to return with bombs if the target could not be found was revoked. They were to be dropped on whatever target the pilot deemed fit.

The German offensive against British cities, especially London (the *Blitz*), provided the British with an opportunity to see what night bombings could achieve with the resources of 1940. The conclusion was reached that the greatest damage was caused by incendiary bombs and that 250 kg high explosive bombs were often insufficient to destroy the machinery and equipment inside industrial buildings (and weight-for-weight the German bombs had more explosive than the British ones). A rough calculation estimated that incendiary bombs had a destructive potential in cities five times greater than high explosive.

Another conclusion was that, given that industrial production ultimately depended on the workforce, the constant bombing of their homes would lead to the death of a great many of them and their families, the destruction of their homes, and the subsequent collapse of morale. This would be one of Bomber Command's missions from now on, one that not only differentiated the British from their American Allies, but also from the Germans; the aim would be to kill as many workers as possible, deliberately, not as a collateral consequence of bombing factories. In this way the destruction of industries would be a collateral effect of the destruction of the workers' districts that surrounded them.

German city centres with their wooden houses and narrow streets became an ideal

1. On 14 May 1940, seventy-one Fairey Battles attacked the bridges that the Germans had thrown over the Meuse and forty were shot down, without a single target being destroyed.

2. Cockpit of a twin-engine *Wellington*.

Formation of *Wellingtons*. It soon became clear that they could not survive daytime missions without an escort.

target for incendiary bombs. Conventional bombs would destroy water pipes, open up buildings to help fires to spread, and hamper the arrival of firefighters. Around 30,000 two kg incendiary bombs, dropped over twenty minutes, were considered necessary to create an uncontrollable urban conflagration. This calculation would prove to be short of the mark. What the British failed to learn from the *Blitz* was that people's morale would not be broken by indiscriminate bombing. They mistakenly believed that the Germans would react differently from the phlegmatic and resolute English.

Although overall strategy was decided at the highest level, Bomber Command operations were the responsibility of its head. In October 1940 Portal was replaced by Peirse, who was more in favour of precision bombing. A month previously Portal had urged his men to bomb cities if the industrial target could not be accurately located. The aircrews were having a hard time of it, due to the limitations of their aircraft, their inadequate training, bad weather conditions, and the poor results being achieved. For each aircraft shot down, six were lost in accidents.

In November, as a reprisal for the bombing of Coventry, Churchill ordered Peirse to attack a German city without any restrictions. The chosen target was Mannheim. On the night of 16 December, 100 aircraft (of the 135 initially planned) reached their target and their bombs killed 34 people. Throughout the winter and the following spring, while the Battle of the Atlantic was in full swing, British efforts were directed, once again unsuccessfully, against oil facilities and naval bases.

1. At the start of the war the *Whitley* was already obsolete and it was soon relegated to other missions.

2. The narrow cockpit of a *Hampden*.

3. The *Hampden* had insufficient defensive armament.

The start of Operation *Barbarossa* changed the situation entirely. On the one hand it brought an end to the *Blitz* and on the other hand it provided Churchill with an unexpected ally. On 7 July he sent a telegram to Stalin promising all possible assistance which, at that time, would be limited to initiating a bombing offensive against Germany. Stalin began to press relentlessly for a second front to be opened, either in France or in Norway.

AIR NAVIGATION

One of the first navigational aid systems used, the "*estimated time of arrival*", was intended to tell the aircrew when they were over the target, using as a reference the last known reliable position in the United Kingdom. The error was often in excess of a hundred kilometres. The only effective aids, when available, consisted of identifying surface references and following them, rarely possible in the skies over northern Europe, or navigating by the stars, something very few navigators were capable of doing and a technique which was also prone to large margins of error.

Churchill did not hesitate to order reprisal attacks on German cities. He always thought of Harris more as a useful tool than as a colleague.

In fact Churchill was in no position to deliver what he promised. In August an exhaustive study (the Butt report) reported that only one out of five bombers came within five miles of the target. Of those who claimed to have released their bombs over the target zone, only one out of four had actually done so, while on moonless nights the ratio dropped to one in fifteen. Overall, over 75 per cent of all bombs were dropped ineffectively. Three months later the situation had worsened: only 15 per cent of the bombers released their bombs within a five mile radius of the target.

Losses due to German defences were growing but those due to accidents were extremely high.

The quality of the aircrews was falling and training was becoming increasingly hurried. In August over

The British twin-engine bombers were very vulnerable to German day fighters.

500 aircraft of Bomber Command were destroyed or severely damaged but only a hundred were replaced. One attack on Berlin ended up with a third of the attacking aircraft not returning.

The fact was that the available equipment was not up to the job. It was necessary to use bigger bombers with heavier bomb payloads, capable of reaching their targets with greater precision. The solution was still a long way off. Navigation systems had scarcely improved after eighteen months of war and technical problems were delaying the entry into service of the three new types of bomber that Bomber Command needed so badly.

The *Stirling*, the only one of the three four-engine bombers originally designed as such, entered service in late 1940. It had good defensive capabilities but a limited ceiling, and its numerous technical problems would not be resolved until well into 1942. The *Halifax* was the development of a previous twin-engine aircraft and the first types were operational by November 1940. Its first mission was in March of the following

OPINIONS

On 7 December 1941, Harris was in Washington negotiating with the Americans regarding the sending of aircraft to the United Kingdom. His impression of his future Allies could not have been more negative: "*These people are not going to fight…they have nothing to fight with. Their arrogance and belief in their superiority are only comparable to the Jews and the Catholics. Their problem is their conviction not only of their superiority but also of our moral, physical and mental ineptitude.*"

Between 1940 and 1941, 2 Group Bomber Command was virtually annihilated in futile missions, whose only objective was to sustain morale and maintain a public image that Britain had the initiative in the war. Even training was highly dangerous; during the war 5,000 men were killed and another 3,100 were injured in training flights. Some units suffered 25 per cent casualties.

1. In 1941 British bombers carried between 15 and 30 per cent incendiary bombs; the Germans between 30 and 60 per cent.

2. The *Wellington* would be used by Coastal Command on anti-submarine missions until the end of the war.

The *Halifax* was a great advance over the twin-engine bombers, but still suffered from many limitations, especially the earlier versions.

year against Le Havre. But it too had a large number of problems that needed solving and it was also hard to fly, so it would never be very popular with aircrews.

The four-engine *Lancaster* was a development of the twin-engine *Manchester* and at last gave Bomber Command the aircraft it needed. This proved to be an aircraft that was capable of carrying out any mission asked of it, but it only entered into service in small numbers in 1942. The *Wellington* dropped 80 per cent of all bombs in 1942. In 1941 nearly 500 four-engine bombers and 4,700 twin-engine bombers were built.

The new aircraft were able to carry heavier bombs. 1,000 and 2,000 kilo bombs started to be made, together with more powerful incendiary bombs, but all this would take time. The planes built in 1941 were intended to make up a total force of 4,000 four-engine bombers by 1943, something that seemed totally unattainable at the time. Negotiations for the supply of American aircraft were even initiated with the United States, but nothing came of them (in any event, even with the addition of American aircraft the figure of 4,000 aircraft would never have been reached).

COMPOSITION OF BOMBER COMMAND

In August 1943 Bomber Command comprised 57 squadrons organized into six groups, 1, 3, 4, 5, 6 and 8. The latter group consisted of pathfinder groups and was responsible for locating and marking targets for the "main force". Group 6 was under Canadian control and its aircrews were formed almost exclusively of Canadians. The aircrews of the rest of the groups came from all corners of the empire, often mixed on board the same aircraft.

The most effective aircraft type was the *Lancaster*, but fewer than half the squadrons were equipped with this type. The remainder were *Halifax* and *Stirling* bombers; their performance was inferior and they accounted for a higher percentage of losses, until they were gradually withdrawn from service. As many as three squadrons of Group 8 would be equipped with twin-engine *Mosquito* aircraft. In 1943 there were still some squadrons flying *Wellingtons*, but by the end of the year they had all been replaced by four-engine bombers.

GERMAN DEFENCES

The *Luftwaffe* deployed a network of radars which would be known as the *Himmelbett* system. With no onboard radar, fighters had to be guided to their target from land, if weather conditions allowed, until the pilot could see the exhaust flames of the enemy bombers and attack visually. Initially Bf 110 C-2, Do 17Z-10, and Ju 88C-2 aircraft were used.

The *Himmelbett* system used two types of radar. Two *Würzburg* sets were combined with one *Freya*. The *Freya* had a range of up to 120 kilometres and could determine the distance and azimuth, but not the altitude, of target aircraft. The *Würzburg* had a range of 50 kilometres and was able to determine altitude accurately. A number of night fighters would group around a radio beacon until directed to a target from land. The so-called *Kammhuber* line stretched from Troyes to the north of Denmark and was up to 200 kilometres deep.

In addition to these classical ground control systems using the *Himmelbett* stations, the night fighters would also use two new tactics in the course of the war:

Zahme Sau (tame boar): Night fighters were guided to the tail end of the bomber streams once their direction had been plotted. In this way they took advantage of their long range, although this often meant landing at an airfield a long way from base. Once on the course of the bomber stream, they used their radar to detect and close in on a four-engine bomber until they had it in visual range.

Wilde Sau (wild boar): This was a tactic using free-ranging night fighters finding targets by sight. Single-engine fighters operating in the area of the target, outside the anti-aircraft fire zone, guided by searchlights and flares or any other light source, including fires. Sometimes high flying bombers were used to drop flares above the target.

The night fighter units were called *Nachtjagdgeschwader* (NJG) and were made up of between 30 and 50 twin-engine fighters, split into three or four *Gruppen*, each with

its own airfield. In August 1943, NJG 1 was based in Holland and Belgium, NJG 3 in Denmark and the north of Germany, NJG 4 in Belgium and the north of France, and NJG 5 in Berlin. NJG 6 was being reorganized in Holland, and the new NJG 6 was being formed in the south of Germany.

FOUR-ENGINE BOMBERS

AVRO LANCASTER

Bomb payload differed greatly according to the mission but it was the only bomber capable of carrying Grand Slam bombs weighing nearly ten tons. Its defensive armament consisted of eight 7.7 mm machine guns in two twin turrets and one quadruple. It was very robust and more manoeuvrable than its American counterparts.

Climb speed: 4.5 m/sec

ARMAMENT

Eight 7.7 mm machine guns

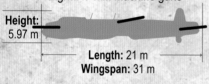

Height: 5.97 m

Length: 21 m
Wingspan: 31 m

RANGE

5 hours

TOP SPEED

445 km/h

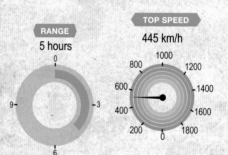

MAXIMUM HEIGHT

8.000 m.

9000
8000
7000
6000
5000
4000
3000
2000
1000
0

AIRCREW

7 men

BOMB PAYLOAD

Up to 6,500 kg of bombs

KG

Empty weight: 16,400 kg

HANDLEY PAGE HALIFAX

Although used in lower numbers than the Lancaster, the Halifax played a significant part in Bomber Command offensives and was the first four-engine aircraft to bomb Germany. Very versatile, nearly 6,200 units were built of which 1,884 were lost in 82,773 missions (a loss rate of 2.2 per cent per mission).

TOP SPEED
450 km/h

MAXIMUM HEIGHT
7.500 m.

Climb speed: 3.8 m/sec

RANGE
3 hours

AIRCREW
7 men

ARMAMENT
Nine 7.7 mm machine guns

BOMB PAYLOAD
Up to 6,000 kg of bombs

Height: 6.3 m

KG
Empty weight: 17,200 kg

Length: 21.8 m
Wingspan: 31.7 m

EQ⊙V

Vicky

SHORT STIRLING

The main drawback was its low ceiling which relegated it to easy targets in 1944, but its payload was high. When it entered service most of the older twin-engine bombers were immediately outclassed.

Climb speed: 4 m/sec

TOP SPEED
450 km/h

MAXIMUM HEIGHT
5.000 m.

ARMAMENT
Eight 7.7 mm machine guns

RANGE
4 hours

KG
Empty weight: 21,200 kg

Height: 6.9 m

Length: 26.6 m
Wingspan: 30.2 m

BOMB PAYLOAD
Up to 6,000 kg of bombs

AIRCREW
7 men

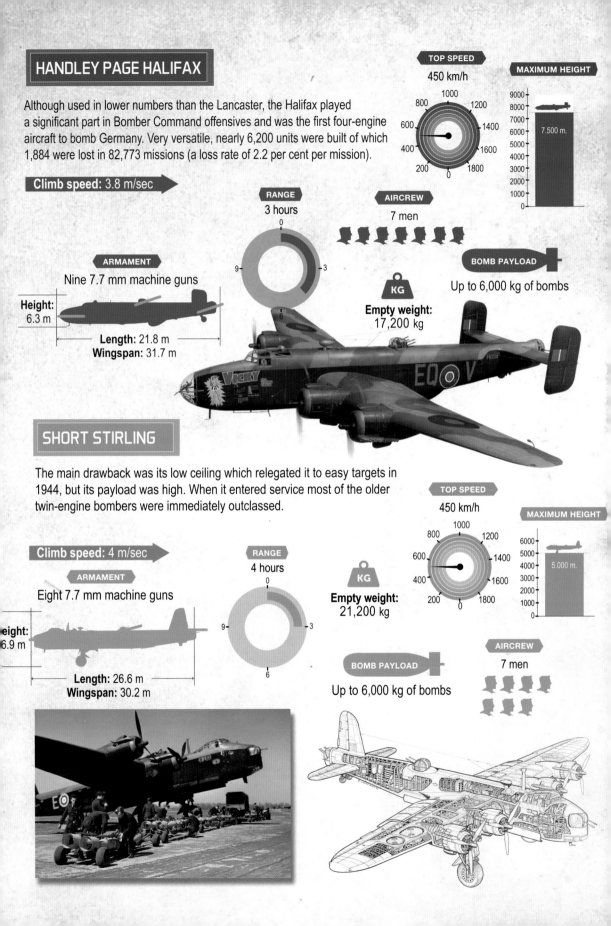

THE GEE SYSTEM

Solutions were starting to be found for the critical problem of navigation. Since by using traditional methods it was proving difficult not only to find a specific target but even an entire city, the fledgling electronics industry was turned to for a solution.

In 1938 scientists had developed an electronic navigation system officially called G and later popularized as *GEE* or *Gee*. Three radio stations transmitted radio signals that could be received by a cathode ray tube onboard an aircraft. At the point of intersection the position could be estimated with a margin of error of between one and six miles. Range was limited to West Germany but it nevertheless represented a considerable step forward. After much debate about how best to use it and a number of trials of questionable success, the system was operative in March 1942.

The Canadians became famous for their lack of discipline but also for their courage and willingness to accept a high percentage of casualties.

At this stage of the war there was no agreement as to what the best way was to penetrate the German defences and destroy or severely damage the target. If bombers attacked in loose formation they were more vulnerable to the *Himmelbett* system but flying was easier and less tiring for the pilots. In close formation the effort required from the pilots was considerable but they could overwhelm the defensive system and suffer very few losses. Once over the target there was no agreement as to what was the best way to mark it with incendiary bombs. And the problem was that they never really knew for sure whether they were over the target and not over some other city altogether.

Churchill, as always, never ceased to push for instant results that were totally beyond the bounds of reality. On 7 November Peirse decided to launch the biggest attack up to that time, with nearly 400 aircraft (but only 40 four-engine bombers), despite the poor weather conditions. In total, 169 aircraft set off for Berlin but only 73 reached the target, destroying 14 houses and killing 9 people. In Cologne they destroyed two houses and killed five people. The rest targeted Mannheim which was completely undamaged. Thirty-seven aircraft were lost, 9 per cent of

The Stirling's low service ceiling was the main reason behind its high loss rate.

BOMBER HARRIS

Born into an aristocratic British family, while still a teenager Arthur Harris emigrated to Rhodesia in 1910, returning during WWI to join the *Royal Flying Corps*. Once the Great War was over he served as the commander of an RAF flying school. He spent some years in the Middle East where he was able to use light bombers to intimidate Arab tribes. In the 1930s he held an important post in the Air Ministry and worked on the development of what he called "the ideal bomber".

In 1939 he commanded the 5th Group, Bomber Command and shortly afterwards became Portal's deputy, until taking command of Bomber Command in February 1942. Intelligent, sharp and aggressive, he showed tremendous resolve and faith in his actions. His relationships with Churchill and the American top brass were not always cordial but they were effective. He had no tolerance for those who did not share his ideas and was openly scornful of their criticism.

He had two major prejudices. First and foremost was his visceral hatred of the Germans, a hatred so great that one of his obsessions was for the bombing to cause the highest number of deaths possible. The second was his conviction that the best way to use heavy bombers was to attack the centre of urban areas. He believed that the destruction of German cities would shorten the war and would save the lives of many allied soldiers (albeit at the cost of the lives of half his aircrews).

In the final stages of the war he came under much scrutiny; Churchill himself distanced himself from Harris and openly criticized his methods and ideas. After the war he moved to South Africa. He died in 1984.

the attacking force, a figure that was logically considered unacceptable. Churchill called Peirse the following morning and ordered him to stop attacks during the winter. In January Peirse was appointed commander of Allied air forces in South-East Asia and the South-West Pacific and, after a brief period in a temporary capacity, Air Marshal Sir Arthur Harris took command of Bomber Command on 22 February.

DIRECTIVE OF SEPTEMBER 1941

"The ultimate aim of an attack on a town area is to break the morale of the population which occupies it. To ensure this, we must achieve two things: first, we must make the town physically uninhabitable and, secondly, we must make the people conscious of constant personal danger. The immediate aim, is therefore, twofold, namely, to produce (i) destruction and (ii) fear of death."

When it entered in service in 1937 the *Blenheim* was an enormous step forward for the RAF. By 1941 its limitations were already apparent.

The United States' entry into the war was a blessing for Churchill and the United Kingdom. After a number of meetings it was soon agreed to set up a US bomber force on British soil in order to attack strategic targets in Germany.

Initially 154 targets were chosen that were considered to be vital, and it was thought that a force of 11,800 heavy bombers would be sufficient to carry out daytime precision bombing missions. Roosevelt approved the construction of 500 aircraft a month to carry out this plan. The US President shared with Churchill the belief that strategic bombing was capable of ensuring victory and he would support the bombing offensive until the end.

But this would take time. The Eighth Air Force was activated on 28 January in the city of Savannah, Georgia, and the first echelon arrived in the United Kingdom on 11 May. In mid-July the first 180 aircraft arrived, of which only 40 were four-engine bombers. Operation *Torch* and the idea that the invasion of France would take place in 1943 diverted part of the US war effort to the production of medium bombers, which were more useful for tactical support.

Harris was not the inventor of area bombing but he did develop it in a spectacular manner. Prior to his arrival, the middle management of the Ministry had been removing restrictions and on 14 February 1942 had issued a directive ruling out communication nodes as priority targets in order to focus on destroying the morale of the civil population, especially factory workers. A list of priority cities was drawn up, pinpointing the most vulnerable historical centres and specifying the estimated tonnage of bombs required for their destruction. Twenty-two million Germans lived in cities with over 100,000 inhabitants. Lord Cherwell sent a report to Churchill in March telling him that in 1943, 10,000 four-engine aircraft could destroy a third of all German homes, which would have a devastating effect on the morale of the population and bring about Germany's surrender.

Harris found himself with a very limited force with which to put his ideas into practice, and called for a minimum of 2,000 four-engine bombers to destroy the twenty cities initially selected as priority targets.

Despite his limited resources he immediately set about showing what he was capable of. He started with a series of night raids on a number of cities, carried out by a little over two hundred bombers, most of them twin-engine *Wellingtons*, which caused a varying amount of damage to the cities of Essen and Cologne and, in particular, Rostock and Lübeck.

1. In 1945 there would be nearly 50,000 air crew and 175,000 ground crew, nearly 20 per cent of the latter being women.

2. A *Hampden* on the ground being made ready for a mission.

3. The *Halifax* became a necessary complement to the *Lancaster*.

1. Briefing session before a mission.

2. Most casualties were suffered by novice aircrews during their first six missions.

The conclusion was reached that, given that the most that an average aircrew could identify at night was a city, all efforts to attack industrial targets with precision bombing were futile and the targets that ought to be identified should simply be urban areas.

But the problems of navigation and target location continued to be enormous. In the case of Rostock, an easy to find city, a little over 20 per cent of the aircraft reached the target. In the case of Essen the figures were laughable. The idea of creating a specific force of pathfinders specialized in finding and accurately marking targets, rather like the German *Kampfgruppe 100*, began to be discussed, but Harris was vehemently opposed to it. He argued that the creation of an elite force would damage the morale of the rest of the main force. He finally had to bow to the pressure and evidence and agreed to such a force being created, but he tried to hinder it whenever he could, by ensuring that it never received the best aircraft and pilots.

Harris came under intense pressure and was strongly criticized from both above and below. So in May he hatched a plan to launch a massive attack on a single city using a thousand bombers in order to demonstrate the validity of his theories and silence his critics once and for all.

LÜBECK

On 28 March 1942, 234 aircraft attacked the Hanseatic City of Lübeck. It was an easy target, hardly defended, with a highly flammable historic city centre, and the RAF was in dire need of a success. Ten *Wellingtons* equipped with the *Gee* radar guided the main formation, dropping flares on the target. They were followed by forty aircraft which dropped incendiary bombs and, shortly afterwards, by the main force, carrying bombs of nearly two tons, flying at a low height on a clear night. Success was total. Over 300 people died and over 3,500 houses were destroyed or seriously damaged. Of the 191 aircraft whose crews claimed to have hit the target, a dozen were lost.

Nearly 600 *Wellington* bombers took part in the attack on Cologne on 30 May 1942.

By 1942 most of the aircrews who had started the war were either dead, POWs, or transferred to desk jobs.

AUGSBURG

The first unit to receive a *Lancaster* was 44 Squadron. On 17 April 1942 this squadron, together with the 97th, would carry out a daring daylight raid on the heart of Germany which would end in disaster. Twelve aircraft (six from each squadron) made the long flight to Augsburg in the south of Germany to attack a submarine engine factory.

Despite the indirect route and various distraction manoeuvres by other units, German fighters shot down four bombers as soon as they were over French soil. The remainder, after a low-level flight, reached the target only to find it defended by heavy flak, which brought down another three aircraft. Each aircraft dropped four 1,000-pound bombs which did enough damage to stop production for several weeks. But the loss of seven out of twelve aircraft and forty-nine out of eighty-five crew members showed just how vulnerable the *Lancaster* was in daytime operations without an escort

3

Harris Gets His Way

The first mission took place on the night of 3-4 March 1942.

Harris's plan, eventually approved by Churchill and Portal, required the cooperation of Coastal Command as well as some training units which had to "lend" a large number of aircraft to reach the sum of one thousand bombers, since Bomber Command only had a little over 400 aircraft operational at that time. The target chosen was Hamburg, easily identifiable due to its proximity to the coast, and the operation was dubbed "*Millennium*". The plan consisted of creating a huge firestorm by dropping a large amount of incendiary bombs in a short space of time in order to pulverize the city centre.

The bad weather gave Hamburg a temporary reprieve as Cologne was chosen as the substitute target. On the night of 30 May, a heterogeneous force of 1,047 bombers took off. Of this total only 868 claimed to have reached the target and dropped 1,445 tons of bombs, two thirds of them incendiary devices. The attack lasted an hour and a half and some 800 tons of bombs actually fell on the city. Around 3,330 buildings were destroyed and another 8,000 damaged. Nearly 500 people were killed and over 5,000 wounded. A total of 40 aircraft were lost; a high but affordable price to pay.

Two nights later another thousand aircraft attack was made on Essen, this time with very poor results (eleven houses destroyed and fifteen fatalities). Late in June another attack on Bremen was launched, again with poor results, and losses rose to 123 bombers over the three missions. Attacks of this nature were called off indefinitely due to the poor results and the high cost in men and machines. The morale of the aircrews was suffering, especially at a time which was proving dramatic for the British Empire, with the loss of Singapore and Tobruk, and with the Germans at the gates of the Caucasus.

QUOTES ATTRIBUTED TO HARRIS

A policeman once stopped him for driving too fast, telling him he could kill someone driving like that. Harris answered: *"Young man, I kill thousands of people every night.*

"There are a lot of people who say that bombing can never win a war. Well, my answer to that is that it has never been tried yet, and we shall see.

"We are going to scourge the Third Reich from end to end. We are bombing Germany city by city and ever more terribly in order to make it impossible for her to go on with the war. That is our object; we shall pursue it relentlessly."

The closing months of 1942 saw a rethinking of tactics and a number of technical innovations. The *Gee* system turned out to be nearly useless since it was successfully intercepted by German stations and began to be replaced by the *Oboe* system and the H2S radar in early 1943. The rapid twin-engine *Mosquito* started to be used in pathfinder units (although in January 1943 there were only 16 operational aircraft).

A *Short Stirling* with its bomb load.

The Eighth US Air Force was deployed much slower than was expected and still had a lot to learn. Stalin was pressing for the immediate opening of a second front and, in order to keep him sweet, the only viable option was a day and night air offensive against industrial targets or simply urban areas. Harris was furious because he was not able to obtain the resources that he considered necessary to launch effective attacks and he complained about what he saw as the slowness of the Americans and the attitude of the Canadian aircrews, who appeared to be fighting a different war to that of the British aircrews.

During 1942 Bomber Command dropped over 37,000 tons of bombs, considerably more than the 23,000 dropped the previous year, but with

On 17 August 1942, twelve *Lancaster* bombers attacked Augsburg by day, causing considerable damage to an engine factory but losing seven aircraft.

During the Ruhr offensive in 1943 the British lost over 600 bombers but the *Luftwaffe* had 283 of their night fighters shot down.

very poor accuracy and at the cost of 2,700 aircraft either shot down or lost in accidents. The effect on the German economy had been minimal; in fact weapons production had increased by 50 per cent. Casualties among the civil population had totalled 4,900; 2 killed for every bomber lost. The only positive effect had been to make the Germans divert aircraft, cannons and ammunition, resources that could be used for other purposes, to air defence.

The truth is that the Allies had no bombing plan other than attacking workers' districts and a limited number of industrial targets in the west of Germany, without being able to evaluate properly the effectiveness of what they were doing. The cost in lives was very high; 14,000 men had lost their

THE H2S RADAR AND THE *OBOE* NAVIGATION SYSTEM

The *Oboe* navigation system (so called because the sound of the transmitter was reminiscent of the musical instrument) consisted of two radar stations, one in Norfolk and the other at Dover, which sent out signals that were received by the aircraft and transmitted back to the transmitter station, enabling the aircraft's position to be established with a fair degree of accuracy. Once the aircraft was over the target, the second station sent out a signal telling the aircrew to drop their bombs. The system was very accurate but had a maximum range of just 270 miles, which meant that targets further away than the Ruhr were not feasible. Also it could only guide one aircraft at a time. The system was later developed and benefited from the entry into service of the *Mosquito*. Its ceiling of 10,000 metres extended the range since it was the curvature of the Earth which set the range limit.

The H2S radar was a transmitter operating in a very narrow waveband. It was able to scan the land below an aircraft, easily identifying urban areas by the type of return signal received. It was immune to interference and had a considerable range. But it needed highly experienced operators to identify correctly accidents of terrain and it was not very accurate. The type Mk III was much more accurate, but it would be a long time before it entered into service in any appreciable numbers as initially it was used for anti-submarine warfare.

lives in Bomber Command in the first three years of the war. The surviving aircrews were starting to feel that their efforts were futile and that the gap between them and the politicians who were taking the decisions, the scientists who were looking for solutions, and the technical people who were developing those solutions, was widening.

PATHFINDERS

On 5 July 1942 Group Captain Donald Bennett, an Australian, took command of the newly formed pathfinder force, initially called *Target Finding Force*. On the 18th he had his baptism of fire on a mission against Flensburg. It was an unfortunate start, since a strong wind sent the formation off course and they attacked a Danish town by mistake, injuring six Danes.

The twin-engine *Mosquito* became the most iconic aircraft of these units, due to its high speed which made it hard to intercept, and its payload capacity. Also its high ceiling, 10,000 metres, meant that the *Oboe* system could be used for more distant targets (the range was set by the curvature of the Earth). Pathfinders, either flying alone or in very small groups ahead of the main formation, located the targets and dropped incendiary bombs to mark them for the following bombers. A total of five pathfinder squadrons were [initially] formed.

As well as incendiary bombs, pathfinders would use various target marking systems, in the form of different types of flares (the Germans dubbed the most spectacular of these "*Christmas trees*"). They would also drop markers along the route to guide the main force.

Pathfinder aircrews flew tours of 45 missions as opposed to the normal 30 flown by other bomber squadrons. Initially only the most veteran aircrews would join the squadrons, but over time casualties began to build up so in later years as many as two thirds of the aircrews came straight from training units while the other third had only flown an average of ten bombing missions before being transferred to pathfinder units.

Unlike in the US Army Air Force, a British pilot could be an NCO and the navigator an officer.

The Casablanca conference sanctioned the development of two independent campaigns, with separate commanders and structures. The Americans would bomb by day and the British by night. Harris felt that he was getting support and continued with his strategy of attacking cities. He believed that the combination of a strategic, unrestricted air offensive against major German cities and the pressure from the Russians on land would deliver the Allies victory in 1944, avoiding the need to invade the continent and so saving many allied lives. In his memoirs he would call this phase "The Great Offensive", although at the time it was never referred to as such.

To achieve his objective he planned a series of attacks which would destroy one city and seriously damage another three every month until September. The Americans were against indiscriminate attacks and wanted to focus on selective raids, so any attempt at collaboration was fruitless.

By spring Bomber Command was finally beginning to reach the aircraft and crew numbers it needed to achieve its objective, with the entry into service of a considerable number of four-engine bombers. In January there were just over 500 four-engine bombers of the three types in service, a number which would continue to increase until the end of the war. The 23,000 men served as aircrew and ground crew totalled 138,000. Over 80 airfields would be required to operate this force by early 1944, plus another 50 for training purposes.

The training of aircrews was an issue that was never properly resolved. Even training schools in the United States were used, but the results were poorer than expected,

Throughout the war the RAF would maintain a rigid class system. Some sources even claim that to be a good officer you had to be middle or upper class and have studied in a 'public' (i.e. private and elitist) school.

in part due to the different training methods but mainly due to the lower cultural level of the British aircrews compared to their American Allies. The British would be joined by men from other Commonwealth countries, such as Canadians, Australians and New Zealanders, who in general had a higher cultural and professional level than their British counterparts.

In the course of the year Harris launched three major offensives, which would be the most important conducted by Bomber Command; against the Ruhr in late spring, against Hamburg in July, and against Berlin in autumn and winter.

The campaign against the Ruhr was simply a continuation of the attacks which had started in May 1940, with the difference that now there would be a large number of four-engine bombers involved, especially *Lancasters*. Bomber Command could now field nearly 800 aircraft, with 75 per cent operability. Each aircraft could drop an average bombload of 3,500 kilos (compared to the 2,400 kilos of the American four-engine bombers). Pathfinder units flew the *Mosquito Mk IX* fitted with the latest versions of *Oboe* and the H2S radar system, although the latter suffered from serious limitations over urban areas.

Harris thought that only one in four of the aircrews were real bombers. The rest only served to be shot at by flak or night fighters.

NIGHT FIGHTERS

The British bombers' worst enemy were the German night fighters; various types of heavily armed twin-engine aircraft fitted with powerful radar.

HEINKEL HE 219 A-0 Uhu

The He 219 was a formidable two-seater night fighter which featured many technological advances, such as ejector seats. Equipped with advanced radar equipment and heavily armed with as many as eight 20 or 30 mm cannons, it was very fast; in fact it was the first German aircraft capable of beating the British *Mosquitoes* for speed. Inexplicably only a few units were built.

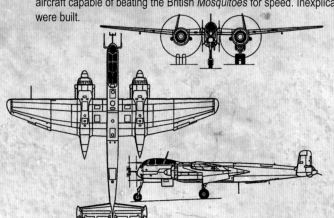

TOP SPEED

670 km/h

MAXIMUM HEIGHT

12.700 m.

RANGE

3 hours

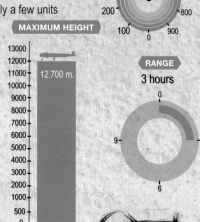

MESSERSCHMITT BF 110 E1

The E type entered into service in 1941 and some later versions had three crew members for night fighter missions. After 1943 the most numerous version began to be built, the G type. It was weighed down by electronic equipment but was nevertheless a very effective aircraft. The most commonly used armament were two 20 mm and two 30 mm cannons, in addition to *Schräge Musik* cannons.

The night fighters' favourite tactic was to close in on the bombers from below, guided by the exhaust glow. Once below their prey, some 50 metres behind, they were invisible. At that moment they would climb and fire a burst at the bomber's underbelly, which tended to be lethal.

MAXIMUM HEIGHT

10.000 m.

TOP SPEED

530 km/h

RANGE

1.5 hours

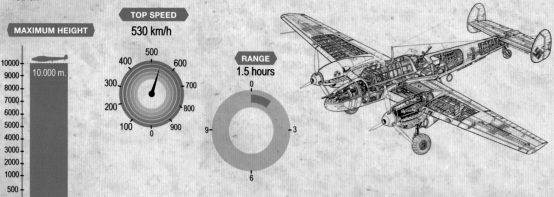

JUNKERS JU 88

The night fighter versions (G and H-1) of the Ju 88 were extremely effective and were responsible for shooting down more night bombers than any other night fighter. In addition to Liechtenstein FuG 202 or 212 radar equipment, they were also fitted with FuG 350 Naxos to detect bombers' H2S signals and with the FuG Flensburg which detected the signals from the Monica tail warning system carried by Mosquitoes. Its normal offensive armament consisted of four MG 151 cannons under the nose and two in *Schräge Musik* configuration.

RANGE
4.5 hours

TOP SPEED
480 km/h

MAXIMUM HEIGHT
9.000 m.

DORNIER DO 217

The first versions were not very effective due to their weight and poor armament. The modifications made to the Do 217N version, with its Liechtenstein radar, several 20 mm cannons mounted in the nose, and four MG 151 *Schräge Musik* cannons firing upwards at an angle of 70°, turned it into an effective night fighter.

TOP SPEED
480 km/h

MAXIMUM HEIGHT
9.000 m.

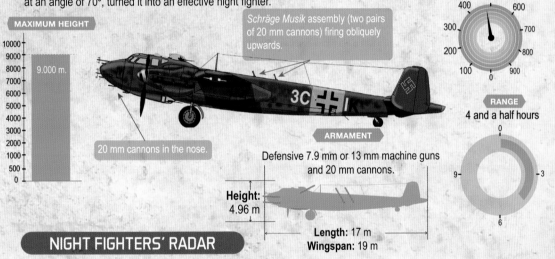

Schräge Musik assembly (two pairs of 20 mm cannons) firing obliquely upwards.

20 mm cannons in the nose.

ARMAMENT
Defensive 7.9 mm or 13 mm machine guns and 20 mm cannons.

Height:
4.96 m

Length: 17 m
Wingspan: 19 m

RANGE
4 and a half hours

NIGHT FIGHTERS' RADAR

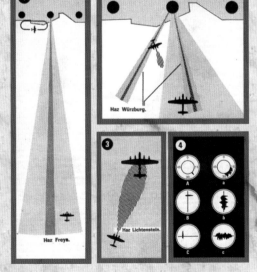

Haz Würzburg.

Haz Lichtenstein.

Haz Freya.

1 Freya radar units were deployed along the coast (the so-called *Himmelbett* line) and had a range of about 160 km. Once they detected an attacker they tracked it as it approached the target.

2 About 50 km from the target the attacker would be detected by *Würzburg* radars. One would track the enemy bomber and another would guide the fighters to intercept. Normally each sector was allocated its own fighters.

3 The fighter was guided towards its target until the interceptor's *Liechtenstein* radar located the bomber. From this point the interceptor closed on the bomber to attack it from behind.

4 The three screens show data from a Liechtenstein radar (on the left is what the fighter's radar operator should see - azimuth, altitude and declination - while on the right we see the effect of the Allies' *Window* radar countermeasure).

Bomber Command HQ was set up in rainy High Wycombe. The operations room was in an underground bunker.

The Ruhr was a very difficult target, due to the urban sprawl, frequent fog and industrial smog, the heavy anti-aircraft defences, and the abundant decoys used by the Germans. The British deployed new target marking systems, electronic countermeasures to jam the *Freya* radars, and warning devices which told bomber aircrews when they had been detected by night fighters' radars. The new *Mk XIV* bombsight could be used even when the aircraft was taking evasive action.

The new offensive started in earnest on the night of 5-6 March with an attack on Essen. Over 440 aircraft dropped over 1,000 tons of bombs, two thirds of them incendiary. It is estimated that 75 per cent fell within a 3 mile radius of the city centre, which was considered to be a great success. Subsequent attacks were less successful and also suffered from a greater dilution of efforts due to attacks on other targets ordered by Churchill, such as Munich and Berlin, leading to considerably less impressive results.

The Ruhr offensive was halted in July, after twenty-eight attacks on the area (interspersed with eighteen attacks on targets far away from the Ruhr). Despite the dispersion, considerable damage was inflicted on urban areas, especially Cologne, Duisburg and Barmen, between May and June. Nearly 70,000 houses were destroyed, leaving nearly 10 per cent of the population homeless. Strategists estimated (highly optimistically) that industrial production had been reduced by 10 per cent. In any event, it was neither a continuous nor concentrated effort and

The *Halifax* carried more incendiary bombs than the *Lancaster*.

the US Eighth Air Force never supported that effort. For the bomber aircrews the experience was dramatic, since they were aware that they were attacking the most heavily defended targets in Germany, with precious little accuracy, under the constant fear of being hit by anti-aircraft fire, coned by searchlights, colliding with another bomber, or even being hit by the bombs of an aircraft flying above them. In that period nearly 900 aircraft were lost in return for some more than questionable results.

On 27 May Harris decided to launch an attack on Hamburg, an attack he had postponed the previous year in favour of his thousand bomber attack. For Operation *Gomorrah*, as the attack was dubbed, the lessons of previous experience and several technical innovations were applied with the aim of causing the highest number of victims possible.

Hamburg was a very good choice of target as far as achieving the degree of devastation that Harris was seeking. It was very easy to find due to its geographical location, had several large shipyards near the city centre, and the historical centre of the city contained a large number of wooden buildings in narrow streets. This attack saw the first use of the *Window* system which succeeded in blinding the German radar.

On the night of 24-25 July, with express approval from Churchill, 728 aircraft took off to attack Hamburg. A pathfinder unit headed the attack, followed over a hundred kilometres behind by the main force. They located their target perfectly under cover of the radar chaos generated by *Window*. In less than an hour they dropped 2,284 tons of bombs on the

ESSEN

The night of 5-6 March saw the start of the Ruhr offensive with an attack on Essen. On a moonless night, eight *Mosquitoes* equipped with *Oboe* radar acted as pathfinders to identify the target. Behind them came 443 bombers which began to release their bombs at nine o'clock. The first to arrive were the *Halifaxes*, followed fifteen minutes later by the *Wellingtons* and, ten minutes after that, the *Stirlings*. Even before the latter had completed their run the *Lancasters* began to arrive, dropping their bombs for around twenty minutes.

The normal bomb payload consisted of one third high explosive bombs and two thirds incendiary. In total, 153 aircraft succeeded in dropping their bombs in a 5 kilometre radius of the target, which was considered to be quite an achievement. Fourteen bombers were lost. The centre of Essen was flattened but damage to industrial facilities was light and the impact on production negligible.

In 1943 Bomber Command lost 4,026 aircraft, 2,823 shot down by the enemy.

city centre, with a density of 17,000 incendiary bombs per square kilometre. However, accuracy was poor, since less than half the bombs fell within a five kilometre radius of the designated target zone. Nevertheless, enormous damage was done to residential areas and in one night nearly 11,000 people died in the many fires that broke out.

The first squadron to receive the *Lancaster* was 44 Squadron. Its first mission was to drop mines in the Gulf of Heligoland on 3 March 1942.

TARGET

Pathfinders tried to release their devices to mark the target as close as possible to the point designated as the objective, which would be an easy to spot geographic feature, such as an intersection, a bridge, or a standout building. It would be logical to expect the bombs to fall in a circle around the designated target but the reality was very different, due to an effect known as "creepback".

For the men responsible for dropping bombs over a blacked-out city, with searchlights sweeping the sky looking for targets and the aircraft shaken by anti-aircraft fire, the prospect of flying on a straight and level course for the long minutes of the final approach to the target was terrifying. The order was to drop bombs when the bombsight was in the *centre* of the target markers, but the temptation to release before reaching that point was enormous. The less resolute would drop their bombs just as they arrived at the markers or even a little before, and the following aircraft would use the fires the first bombs had started as their target marker. Inevitably the bombs started to fall increasingly further away from (before) the actual target.

When this tendency was seen to be inevitable, targets began to be marked beyond the urban zone that was to be destroyed, thereby factoring in the creepback effect. The area actually bombed, assuming that most aircraft would arrive grouped together, changed from being a theoretical circle to being spindle-shaped. This was known as offset marking.

The Eighth Air Force attacked the city for the next two days, suffering heavy losses at the hands of aggressive daytime fighters and increasing the tally of victims by a further 500. But the worst was yet to come. On the night of 27-28 July, another 729 aircraft dropped 2,326 tons of bombs on the most populated residential areas of Hamburg. The effect of 1,200 tons of incendiary bombs falling in less than an hour in an area of less than 4 square kilometres, combined with the extreme dryness of the atmosphere and the unusually hot weather, was devastating. Amid the uncontrollable firestorm, with temperatures reaching over 800 °C, the super-heated air formed an actual tornado of fire. Many inhabitants died inside bomb shelters due to a lack of oxygen, which had been consumed by the fire. Around 18,500 people died and over 20 square kilometres of the city was incinerated.

CORKSCREW

One tactic used against night fighters by *Lancaster* crews was called *corkscrew*. If the tail gunner spotted a fighter closing in from behind, he would warn the pilot with the order *"Fighter to port. Corkscrew port. Go!"* whereupon the pilot would make a sharp turn to port while diving at high speed for several hundred metres. Then he would make another sharp turn to starboard before levelling off. These turns could be linked together into a descent of over a thousand metres. With luck the *Lancaster* would shake off the attacking fighter. Only the *Lancaster* was sturdy enough to withstand these manoeuvres but for the crew it must have been a harrowing experience.

Harris launched another two attacks, on the nights of 29 July and 2 August, which increased the tally of victims to around 40,000: 60 per cent of the buildings were destroyed and 900,000 people were left homeless. The cost for Harris was very acceptable; 87 aircraft in all the raids (2.5 per cent), with a total of 3,095 missions flown and 9,000 tons of bombs dropped.

FIRES

Experience had shown that the massive use of incendiary bombs was the best way to destroy cities. It was calculated that around 25,000 incendiary bombs per square mile were necessary to create an uncontrollable fire. But it was also necessary to use high explosive bombs to blow out windows and walls in order to allow the fire to propagate and to impede and intimidate firefighters. In this respect bombs with time delay fuses which exploded between three and ten minutes after hitting the ground were also very useful.

At the beginning of the war the most common incendiary device was the 4-pound magnesium bomb. These would be complemented by 30-pound bombs with a higher penetration capacity containing a mixture of white phosphorous and petroleum jelly.

Preparing for take off.

This deadly attack on the Germans had a dramatic effect. Priority was given to the construction of fighters to defend the skies over the *Reich*, new tactics were developed for night fighters, and there was a considerable increase in the number of anti-aircraft guns, all of which took resources away from other fronts. Harris was euphoric and claimed that if things continued as they were, Germany would be defeated by the end of the year. But the German ability to recover exceeded all expectations. It has been calculated that real losses were equivalent to 12 per cent of the city's production and that by the end of August the shipyards were once again operating at 70 per cent of their capacity.

On 28 March 1942, 234 aircraft attacked Lübeck in three waves. They destroyed 60 per cent of the historical city centre and killed 312 people.

The Quebec conference in August left it in no doubt that the priority of the allied air offensive was the destruction of the *Luftwaffe,* in order to achieve air superiority prior to the invasion. But only the Eighth Air Force appeared to take this on board. Harris and Bomber Command were playing in another league, especially after the enthusiasm aroused by the attack on Hamburg. Harris was convinced that the war could be won without a costly invasion through the systematic destruction of German cities. Late in the year he submitted a document explaining that the destruction of 50 per cent of the largest German cities would create such devastation that surrender would be inevitable by April 1944 at the very latest. Churchill had reasons to be optimistic and allowed Harris to proceed with his plans, giving him his total support, even to the point of bypassing the chain of command.

THE *WINDOW* SYSTEM

Window (or chaff as it is called today) was designed to jam German radars. It consisted of dropping large quantities of strips of paper of a certain size (30 cm long by 1.5 cm wide) with one side covered in aluminium. The aim was to swamp radar screens with a huge number of returns, causing the screens to blur. The Germans had a similar system called *Düppel*, but had not dared to use it for fear that the British would discover it and use it against them. The RAF had waited to use it for the same reason, until they had a new radar system which could beat it. Each aircraft dropped bundles of 2,000 strips, at a rate of one bundle a minute, thereby creating an enormous screen which enemy radar could not penetrate.

SOME FIGURES

During the Ruhr offensive, Bomber Command flew 18,500 missions and lost 872 aircraft (an acceptable 4.7 per cent) while 16 per cent were grounded by various types of faults. Around 58,000 tons of bombs were dropped, more than in the whole of 1942, and more than the Germans had dropped on Great Britain in 1940 and 1941 combined.

In late April 1942, Rostock was attacked for two nights. Around 60 per cent of the historic city centre was either destroyed or damaged and 216 inhabitants lost their lives.

4

Operation *Chastise*

The idea of collapsing German military industry through selective attacks on vital facilities led to one of the most spectacular operations of the war. The large reservoirs of the Ruhr Valley supplied water not only to the people living there but also to industry and major hydroelectric plants. Already before the war three large dams had been identified as key structures in the Ruhr Valley; the Möhne and Sorpe dams on the Rhine and the Eder Dam on the river of the same name which feeds into the Fulda. The first two supplied 75 per cent of the hydroelectric power in the Ruhr Valley, so their neutralization would have dramatic consequences for industry.

As early as 1938, ways to attack the dams were being studied but it soon became clear that they were very difficult targets to attack from the air. Firstly they were very small targets and secondly it would need a large amount of explosives to destroy them. At that time it was a technical impossibility.

BARNES NEVILLE WALLIS

Born in 1887, the son of a doctor, Wallis studied engineering and was soon to make a name for himself by designing a very light, solid structure known as a geodetic airframe, which was used in the construction of the R100 airship in 1930. While working for the company *Vickers-Armstrong* he designed several aircraft using that structure to give them great strength and rigidity for little weight, aircraft such as the *Wellesley*, the *Warwick*, the *Windsor* and, most especially, the *Wellington*.

Seeking a way of attacking targets protected by anti-torpedo nets, he designed a bomb which would bounce on the surface of the water until it reached its target, whereupon it would sink and then explode, thereby maximizing damage. This invention would be the weapon used to attack the Ruhr dams. He would also design the biggest bombs to be dropped in the war, the *Tallboy*, weighing in at 6 tons, and the *Grand Slam* weighing a massive 10 tons, which could only be carried by the *Lancaster*.

After the war he would continue to work on aeronautical projects; his swing-wing supersonic aircraft was perhaps his most outstanding project. He was married for fifty-two years. He died at the age of 92 and his widow, Molly, survived him by just one year.

OPERATION CHASTISE: THE DAMBUSTERS

The specially modified *Lancasters* reached their targets after an eventful flight at very low height. Once the targets were located they made a number of passes until they succeeded in getting into the right position for releasing their bombs.

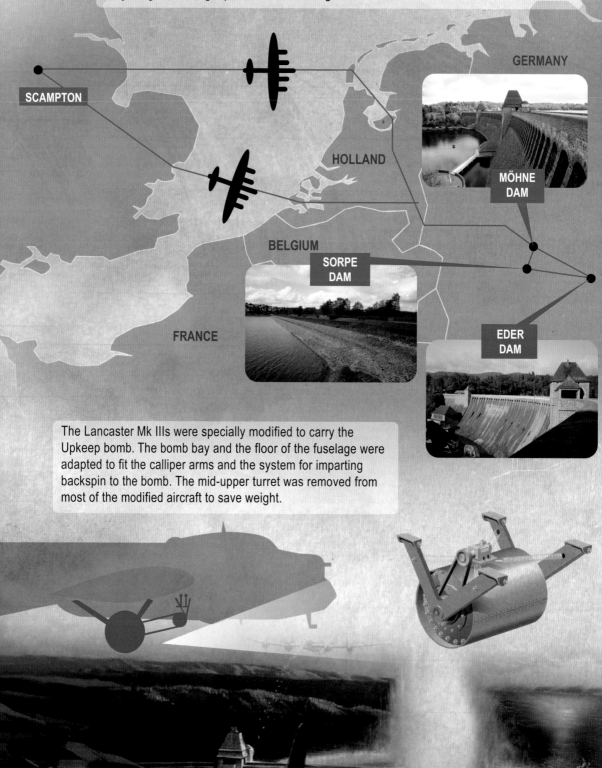

GERMANY

SCAMPTON

HOLLAND

MÖHNE DAM

BELGIUM

SORPE DAM

FRANCE

EDER DAM

The Lancaster Mk IIIs were specially modified to carry the Upkeep bomb. The bomb bay and the floor of the fuselage were adapted to fit the calliper arms and the system for imparting backspin to the bomb. The mid-upper turret was removed from most of the modified aircraft to save weight.

PROFILE OF THE ATTACK

▷ The bomb was dropped with backspin, and after bouncing a number of times on the surface of the water it would strike the dam and sink before exploding at the depth pre-set by a hydrostatic device. In this way the shock wave created in the water by the explosion of *Upkeep*'s three and a half tons of high explosive would wreak the maximum damage on the dam.

► Two spotlights were used, one under a wing and one under the fuselage, each shining at a precise angle so that the beams would converge on the surface of the water when the aircraft was at the right height.

► In order to determine the bomb release point for the Möhne and Eder dams, the two towers at either end of the dams were used as reference points. The bomb aimer used a wooden bombsight which told him it was time to release the bomb when the two towers were aligned with the pins on each end of the device.

THE PRICE IN MEN AND AIRCRAFT

Of the 153 crew members who took part, 56 perished. Of the 30 Canadians involved, 14 were killed.

RETURNED	FAILED TO RETURN	ATTACKED A DAM	REACHED A DAM	BROKE A DAM	FAILED TO ATTACK	WAVE

AJ-G (George)	AJ-M (Mother)	AJ-P (Peter)	AJ-A (Apple)	AJ-J (Johnny)	AJ-L (Leather)	AJ-Z (Zebra)	AJ-N (Nancy)	AJ-B (Baker)
1	1	1	1	1	1	1	1	1
Gibson's aircraft. Attacked the Möhne Dam	Shot down after attacking the Möhne Dam	Failed to reach the Möhne Dam	Damaged the Möhne Dam and was shot down on the way home	Its bomb caused the Möhne Dam to burst	Hit the Eder Dam, without any apparent effect	Its bomb bounced over the Eder Dam. Shot down on the way home	Hit the Eder Dam and caused a breach	Crashed on hitting a power cable on the way to the target

AJ-T (Tommy)	AJ-E (Easy)	AJ-K (King)	AJ-H (Harry)	AJ-W (Willie)	AJ-C (Charlie)	AJ-O (Orange)	AJ-S (Sugar)	AJ- (York)
2	2	2	2	2	3	3	3	3
Hit the Sorpe Dam, without apparent damage	Crashed on hitting an electricity power pylon	Shot down by flak over the sea	Lost bomb on outward flight after clipping a wave	Damaged by flak; aborted attack	Shot down by flak	Attacked and hit the Ennepe Dam, without damaging it	Crashed after hitting treetops	Failed to find target due to fog

AJ-F (Freddy)
3
Hit the Sorpe Dam without causing any appreciable damage

AVRO *LANCASTER*

The four-engine *Avro Lancaster*, designed by Roy Chadwick's team as a direct evolution of the twin-engine *Avro Manchester*, became the most iconic British bomber of the war. It was certainly an impressive aircraft. It was very sturdy and was highly manoeuvrable for an aircraft of its weight and size. Its capacious bomb bay enabled large, heavy bombs to be carried, including the *Grand Slam* which weighed close to 10 tons. It had a range of 1,600 kilometres although with a more usual bomb payload of between 6 and 8 tons its range was greater. It would be the allied bomber with the highest payload of the war.

One of its weaknesses was its defensive armament compared with the American four-engine bombers, since the *Lancaster* only had eight 7.7 mm machine guns in three turrets, two twin and one quadruple. One of the reasons for this was the lack of available aircrew, which was normally limited to seven members: pilot, co-pilot (until 1942, when co-pilot duties were performed by the flight engineer), navigator/bomb-aimer, radio-operator/front gunner, upper gunner, and tail gunner. It was easy to fly and quickly became very popular among aircrews.

Its high payload and manoeuvrability meant that it was the bomber chosen for all the most hazardous and demanding missions, which is reflected in a high number of losses when compared with other [American] four-engine bombers. A total of 6,750 *Lancasters* would be built during the war, suffering a loss rate of 3.9 per cent per mission (nearly half that of the *Halifax*). They flew over 159,000 missions and dropped nearly 620,000 tons of high explosive bombs and over 50 million incendiary bombs. In the course of the war 3,345 aircraft and 21,751 crew members were lost.

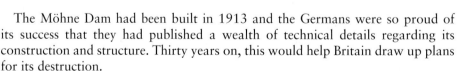

The Möhne Dam had been built in 1913 and the Germans were so proud of its success that they had published a wealth of technical details regarding its construction and structure. Thirty years on, this would help Britain draw up plans for its destruction.

Barnes Wallis, an outstanding engineer at *Vickers-Armstrong*, succeeded in finding a technical solution to the problem of how to destroy the dams using the resources at his disposal. After ruling out a number of projects involving huge bombs, he reached the conclusion that the only way to breach the dams was to detonate a high-power explosive charge at the base of the dam, in order to take advantage of the amplification effect of shock waves under water. The best way, and practically the only way at that time, to place an explosive charge at the base of the dam was by using a cylindrical bomb which would bounce on the surface of the water until it reached the dam, where it would sink and detonate at the required depth.

The design and development process of that bomb has been described in many publications and a now classic film, so suffice it to say that, finally, after much trial and error, a cylindrical bomb, given the codename *Upkeep*, was developed. It resembled an enormous four and a half ton barrel which would need to be carried by a specially modified *Lancaster* bomber. The bomb would be spun backwards just before being released at a specific height and speed and, skimming across the water like a stone, it would bounce towards the dam. There it would sink before exploding at the required depth. The water shock wave would do the rest.

Once the technical problem had been resolved, the next step was to convince Harris that the project was worthwhile. Harris initially rejected it, considering it

1. Airmen of the recently formed 617 Squadron studying their mission.

2. *Upkeep.* Barnes Wallis thought that a single impact in the centre would be enough to destroy a dam.

3. Gibson had his dark side. An undisputed leader, many of his subordinates described him as arrogant, intolerant, and conceited.

A badge of 617 Squadron, a squadron which was to become legendary.

to be just one more hare-brained scheme that he was regularly presented with as the way to win the war. But the idea reached the ears of Portal and Churchill who were both convinced that it might work, so Harris was ordered to go ahead with the plan. The raid would take place in the spring of 1943, at the height of the Ruhr offensive, when the reservoirs would be full and the weather favourable.

Harris continued to be obstructive. It was necessary to create a squadron which would receive special training for this one mission and Harris was opposed to choosing elite aircrews. Finally, a fair number of experienced pilots were assembled (with at least one 30-mission tour completed, in some cases two), but for some of the crew members this was to be their first mission. To command the new squadron, number 617, a veteran and charismatic pilot, Guy Gibson, was chosen.

Late in March 1943 a rigorous and intensive training process was set in motion, without even Gibson himself knowing what the real target would be (nearly everyone thought they would be bombing the battleship *Tirpitz*). Special emphasis was placed on low-level night flying over water, the best way to reach the target and attack it. Finally, the order to proceed with the attack was given on the night of 16-17 May, taking advantage of good meteorological conditions. The operation was given the codename *Chastise*.

On the afternoon of the 16th Gibson informed his men of the details of the attack and what the real target was. Barnes Wallis attended the briefing and explained the technical details of the bomb and its effect on the dam. Three dams were chosen as the primary targets – the Möhne, Eder and Sorpe dams - and another three were secondary targets - Lister, Ennepe and Diemel. Three groups of three aircraft would take off first and head for the first two primary targets, followed by a group of five aircraft which would head for the Sorpe Dam. Two and a half hours later the five remaining aircraft were to take off, acting as a reserve force.

At 21h 28 the first aircraft took off, followed by the other components of the first two waves. They headed towards the English Channel, flying at a very low height.

The aircraft made use of visual references (canals, towns) to navigate by, flying below German radar cover. But that exposed them to light anti-aircraft fire. One of the *Lancasters* was shot down over Holland and another clipped a wave and lost its bomb but was able to return to base at RAF Scampton. A third was shot down a few kilometres short of the target (the bomb was recovered by the Germans intact).

THE *DAMBUSTERS*

The four-engine *Lancaster Mk III* was specially modified for this mission. A structure was installed in the bomb bay to hold the bomb, which hung partly below the fuselage until ready to be dropped. A belt drive spun the bomb backwards at 500 rpm before it was launched. The bomb was the heaviest ever used by the RAF at that time. It weighed four and a half tons of which some 3,200 kilos was *Torpex* explosive.

In order to save weight the mid-upper turret of the *Lancaster* was removed. New transmission equipment was installed and two ingenious but simple systems were used to ensure that the bomb was released at the right height and distance. For height, two powerful spotlights were fitted to the underside, with beams that would converge on the surface of the water ahead of the aircraft to tell the crew that they were at the right height for their bombing run. For distance, a triangular aiming device was used which used the towers of the dams as reference points to tell the bomb aimer when the aircraft was in position to drop the bomb. At Sorpe, which had no towers, the bomb was dropped conventionally, without any backspin.

Gibson reached his target, Möhne, and made a first dummy run over the dam. Anti-aircraft guns began to fire as Gibson circled round to make his attack. At 232 mph and at a height of 20 metres, the bomb aimer released *Upkeep* which, after bouncing three times, struck the dam and sank. The subsequent explosion sent up a column of water over 300 metres into the air, but the dam held.

The Sorpe Dam had no towers to serve as reference points to judge the bomb release point and was attacked in a more conventional manner to little effect.

GUY GIBSON

Guy Penrose Gibson was born in India in 1918 and joined the RAF when he was 18 years old. At the beginning of the war he was flying *Hampdens,* in which he completed his first tour of missions. After a brief period as a flying instructor he asked to be transferred to an operational unit and was sent to Fighter Command where he flew *Blenheims* and *Beaufighters* on night fighter missions. In ninety-nine sorties he shot down three aircraft. He was then given command of 106 Squadron of Bomber Command with which he completed his second tour of duty, having established a reputation as being an aggressive and courageous flyer with strong leadership capabilities.

In March 1943, at the age of 24, he took command of the newly created 617 Squadron and tried to recruit as many members of his former unit, 106 Squadron, as he could. After the raid on the dams, for which he earned the Victoria Cross, he took part in a fundraising tour of North America and wrote a successful book on the Dambuster raid entitled *Enemy Coast Ahead.* Against the wishes of his superiors he returned to active service in September 1944, flying a *Mosquito* in a pathfinder role. He failed to return from a sortie on 20 September.

The second *Lancaster* completed its attack but, having been hit by anti-aircraft fire, dropped its bomb late. The bomb overshot the dam and hit a hydroelectric power station further down the valley, shortly before the aircraft crashed in flames. Gibson flew parallel to and slightly ahead of the third aircraft as it made its bombing run with all its lights on in order to draw away anti-aircraft fire. Although the bomb hit its target the dam held. The two aircraft that had dropped their bombs then flew with the next aircraft as it made its approach. The third explosion finally breached the dam.

Two aircraft headed home while Gibson, together with the aircraft that still had bombs, set a course for the Eder Dam. This was a very difficult target because the surrounding hills meant that the bombers had to swoop down from a height of over 300 metres in a very short distance. After making a number of runs without achieving the right distance and height, two of the aircraft hit the

1. The spotlights told the pilot when he was at the right height for his approach.

2. Recreation of the attack with a *Lancaster* overflying the Eder Dam.

3. Gibson's faithful dog, Nigger, was run over and killed shortly before Gibson took off. Visibly affected, Gibson asked for his dog to be buried when his squadron would be over the target. Nigger's grave is still well cared for to this day.

target and the dam was breached. A third aircraft was severely damaged by the shock wave from one of the bombs which hit the dam and was finally shot down by anti-aircraft fire.

The Sorpe Dam was attacked by a single aircraft in the second wave, since of the five aircraft originally given the Sorpe as their target, two were shot down and another two had to return home due to various problems. The *Lancaster* that did hit the dam was a reserve aircraft (the original one having developed a fault just before take-off) and was not equipped in the same way as the other bombers, so the bomb had to be dropped conventionally. After nine attempts (fortunately there was no anti-aircraft defence) the pilot finally got into the right position and hit the target. But unlike the attacks on the other two dams, the explosion only damaged the crest, not the structure.

About to release the bomb over the Möhne.

Gibson explaining the attack on his return.

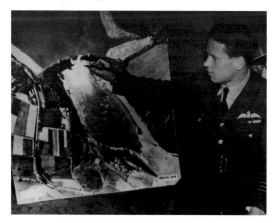

Of the five reserve aircraft, two were shot down, one attacked the Sorpe unsuccessfully, another the Ennepe, also unsuccessfully, and the last one, which should have attacked the Diemel Dam, was unable to find the target in the fog and returned with the bomb still on board. The last aircraft to return home landed at RAF Scampton at 06h15. Eight aircraft, with 56 crew members on board, failed to return. Wallis, while satisfied with the success of his bomb, was dismayed by the loss of aircrew lives. Years later he would say. *"If I'd known that 56 young men would die I would never have started the project. It was pointless and they were so young and brave."*

At the end of the day the attack was more spectacular than effective. The Germans were taken completely by surprise since they had never expected an attack of that nature. The damage to the Möhne and Eder

At 00h56 Gibson sent the much awaited signal, Nigger, which meant that the Möhne Dam had been breached.

dams was considerable. Both dams had enormous breaches and the valleys downstream were totally flooded. The floodwater destroyed several hydroelectric plants and over 1,300 people perished (more than half of them were forced labourers from occupied countries). Speer [Hitler's architect] was dumbfounded, but the rebuilding work began immediately. Over 7,000 workers were transferred from other sites (most from the work on the *Atlantikwall*) to work on the dams and anti-aircraft defences were strengthened considerably around the dams.

By September the Möhne Dam was operational again, albeit with a restricted capacity, followed shortly afterwards by the Eder Dam, although this dam was not fully repaired until after the war. The overall effect of the attack on industrial production was far less than was hoped for due to the rapid repairs made, but it did of course divert considerable efforts and resources to the reconstruction of the damaged dams and, in particular, to the protection of all Germany's many dams.

In the United Kingdom there was much celebration and the effect on morale was considerable at a time when good news was in short supply. Harris himself, once he had got over his misgivings about this type of operation, was

One of the targets of the Tallboy; a V2 launch site at St Omer.

EARTHQUAKE BOMBS

Developed during 1943, the 12,000-pound *Tallboy* bomb had the perfect ballistic shape to reach a high impact speed, combining high explosive capacity with the penetrative power of an armour piercing projectile. It was dubbed "earthquake bomb" due to its effects after impact. Its ability to explode after having penetrated to a considerable depth meant that the shock waves produced by its huge explosive charge had a tremendously destructive effect over a wide radius, even without the need for a direct hit.

On 14 March 1945 a 10-ton *Grand Slam* bomb destroyed the Bielefeld viaduct between Hamm and Hanover. Until the end of the war another forty of these monstrous devices were dropped on especially difficult or well-protected targets. It was basically a scaled-up version of the *Tallboy* and only the *Lancaster* could carry it.

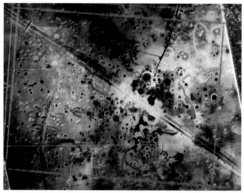

The effects of the *Grand Slams* dropped on and around the Bielefeld viaduct.

ecstatic and, as was his habit, effusively congratulated the aircrews, who received various medals. However, the price had been very high, since nearly half the attacking force (eight out of seventeen aircraft) had been lost. At a dinner for the aircrews in London on 22 June at which medals were awarded, the menu was headed *Dam Busters*, a term which was to became immortalized.

In the autumn the squadron unsuccessfully attacked the Dortmund-Ems Canal with conventional bombs but shortly after, on 16 December, the squadron scored a spectacular success when nine *Lancasters*, using the new stabilized bombsight, destroyed a V1 launch site at Abbeville, with a margin of error of less than 90 metres.

In a high precision raid on 8 February 1944 the unit destroyed a *Gnome-Rhône* engine factory at Limoges, after the target had been marked from a *Lancaster* flying at a height of 80 metres. Twelve aircraft dropped five of the new 6-ton *Tallboy* bombs and a number of 500 kg devices.

PRECISION RAIDS

One very controversial attack took place when four brand new *Mosquitoes* belonging to 105 Squadron attacked Gestapo Headquarters in Oslo on 25 September 1942. At the time it was the longest ever mission in terms of distance, a round trip of 1,800 kilometres, flying at an altitude of thirty metres to avoid detection. Two Fw 190s intercepted the attackers before they reached the target and only two *Mosquitoes* made it to Oslo. Each aircraft dropped four 500-pound bombs, three of which exploded in the Gestapo building, which was seriously damaged. But over eighty Norwegians lost their lives in the immediate vicinity, which provoked a protest from the Norwegian government in exile.

Mosquitoes attacking at rooftop height.

OBJECTIVE *TIRPITZ*

Another of Squadron 617's successes was the attack that sank the battleship *Tirpitz*. The ship had become the *bête noire* of the Royal Navy; while it had never dared engage surface units, it had succeeded in diverting an enormous amount of resources which were much needed in other theatres, without once venturing out from its anchorages in the Norwegian fjords. After being seriously damaged after a raid by midget submarines in the Kaa fjord, it was patched up and preparations began to be made for it to sail to the Baltic where repairs would be completed.

On 3 April it was attacked by aircraft from six different aircraft carriers which inflicted enough damage to require another three months of repairs. In another attack by twenty-seven *Lancasters* from Russian airfields near Archangel on 15 September, the *Tirpitz* received a direct hit from a *Tallboy*, causing serious damage. A few weeks later it was taken to Tromso to act as a static battery since by now any definitive repair had been ruled out.

On 12 November, thirty-two *Lancasters* of Squadrons 9 and 617, armed with *Tallboy* bombs, took off from bases in Scotland, 1,600 kilometres away from their target (Operation *Catechism*). The aircraft were specially prepared for the mission; they were fitted with extra fuel tanks and their cockpit armour and mid-upper turret had been removed. A serious error of coordination between the *Kriegsmarine* and the *Luftwaffe* had enabled the *Lancasters* to press home the attack without opposition. Of the twenty-eight *Tallboys* dropped in the space of around ten minutes, three hit the ship. This time the damage was irreparable. The *Tirpitz* began to heel dramatically before turning turtle.

A few days later an attack against the Anthéor viaduct failed, but it became clear that a precision attack was possible given the right resources and conditions.

On 8 June 1944 the Saumur tunnel was attacked with *Tallboy* bombs. Twenty-two aircraft dropped these nearly 6-ton bombs from heights of between 2,500 and 3,500 metres, achieving eighteen hits at no more than 200 metres from the tunnel. The leading aircraft of the squadron had previously marked the target from a height of 150 metres.

A *Tallboy* just released from a *Lancaster* on its way to its target.

The Saumur tunnel, destroyed by earthquake bombs.

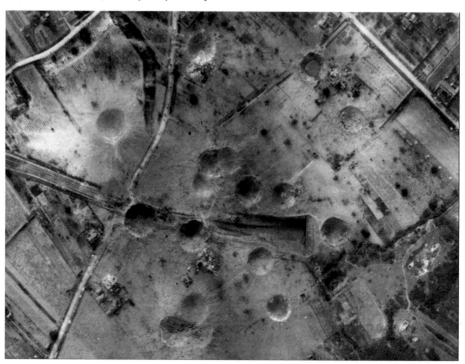

5

Battle of Attrition

In the second half of 1943, the losses suffered by allied bombers grew alarmingly and they proved unable to wrest the *Reich's* initiative over the skies away from the *Luftwaffe*.

Harris finally decided to launch his announced offensive against Berlin, which started on the night of 23-24 August. He had been waiting for a period of long moonless nights and the right weather conditions. Berlin was a long way away and heavily defended. A nearly seven-month long period of raids ensued in which nineteen major attacks would be made on the capital of the Reich and over 30,000 tons of bombs would be dropped on the target area.

One of Bomber Command's main problems was not knowing with any accuracy the extent of the damage inflicted and its impact on the enemy.

In the first attack, conducted by 719 aircraft carrying over 1,800 tons of bombs, 8.7 per cent of the bombers were lost, a very high price to pay. In exchange for these losses over 800 people were killed and 2,600 houses destroyed, but the bombs fell over a very wide area. Ten pathfinders were lost, although most of the losses were suffered by the *Stirlings*, which flew at a lower altitude and so were easier prey for night fighters, flying for the first time on *Wilde Sau* missions. In total 20 *Lancasters* were lost (out of 335), 25 *Halifaxes* (out of 251), and 17 *Stirlings* (out of 124).

THE PEENEMÜNDE RAID

On 17 August 1943, nearly 600 aircraft took off to attack a target which had hitherto been ignored; a German research centre on the Baltic island of Peenemünde. Over 1,800 tons of bombs were dropped with remarkable accuracy by 560 aircraft, causing tremendous damage to the facility

where the first V2 missiles were being developed (unfortunately killing over 500 Polish forced labourers who were working there). Forty aircraft were lost but the centre was never rebuilt, and the facilities dedicated to missile development were scattered among hidden locations in the heart of the *Reich*.

DE HAVILLAND *MOSQUITO*

The *De Havilland Mosquito* was one of the most memorable aircraft of the Second World War. It was designed by private initiative in 1938 as a light bomber and reconnaissance aircraft, with the idea of it being so fast and flying at such a height that it could do without defensive weapons. In order to save on strategic materials such as aluminium it was built almost entirely of wood. But initially the Air Ministry showed no interest in it whatsoever.

After the start of the war an order for fifty units was placed, the first of which flew in November 1940. It caused a tremendous sensation since it was faster than a fighter and nearly as manoeuvrable. It was immediately pressed into service as an impossible-to-intercept reconnaissance aircraft and a year later a bomber version entered in service to replace the obsolete *Blenheim*.

The *Mosquito* soon became the ideal pathfinder aircraft. Fighter, fighter-bomber, anti-shipping and night fighter versions were developed; in total there were over thirty different versions totalling nearly 7,800 units in all. In some countries they remained in service until the sixties.

The empty weight was 7,250 kg with a top speed of 615 km/h (Mk IV version) thanks to its two *Rolls-Royce Merlin* engines and its smooth lines. The aircrew (pilot and navigator) sat side-by-side in an armoured cockpit. The service ceiling was 11,000 metres. As a bomber it could carry up to two tons of bombs, including one of 1,800 kilos. The night fighter version was armed with four 20 mm cannons and four 7.7 mm machine guns.

A week later, a second attack resulted in similar losses and very poor results, due to the H2S radar working so badly that some bombers dropped their bombs over 45 kilometres away from the designated target. The most vulnerable aircraft were the *Stirlings* and the *Halifaxes*, so on 3 September only *Lancasters* took part. The result was similar; once again 7 per cent of the four-engine bombers were lost in exchange for minimal damage to Berlin. The proper identification of the target became an almost insoluble problem unless the night was clear enough for visual bombing, in which case the bombers would be terribly vulnerable to enemy fighters.

In the autumn of 1943 only 20 per cent of the bombs dropped using radar fell within a radius of 8 kilometres of the target.

NIGHT FIGHTER TACTICS

The German night fighters had two main ways of attacking; either closing in from behind or, when the aircraft was fitted with *Schräge Musik*, attacking from below in order to fire at the underbelly of the bomber.

Guided by radar the fighter would close in until the pilot either located his target using the radar itself or visually. The exhaust flames from the engines tended to be the first thing to give a bomber's position away.

Firing cone.

When attacking from below the fighter would approach from some distance below and then climb steeply. With the first bursts the crew would try to knock out the bomber's tail gunner, the night fighter's most feared enemy. Next the fighter would fire at the wings in order to hit and set fire to the bomber's fuel tanks.

Blind spot for bomber crews and defensive fire.

Using *Schräge Musik* the fighter would sneak up under the bomber's underbelly, taking advantage of the blind spots of the aircraft's turrets. They also shot at the wings, hoping to hit the fuel tanks.

Schräge Musik

The system known as *Schräge Musik* proved to be highly effective. It consisted of a set of two or four 20 mm cannons (later even 30 mm) in the rear of the cockpit, aiming obliquely upwards, to attack enemy bombers from below.

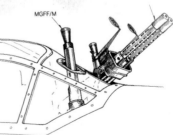

MGFF/M

Harris decided to look for easier targets and in October he scored a notable success at Kassel, where the four-engine bombers were surprisingly accurate and devastated the city, killing 6,000 people. Nevertheless, as occurred in Hamburg, two months later industrial production had returned to 90 per cent of its level prior to the attack. And the price had been high for the Allies: forty-three aircraft were lost, 7.6 per cent of the attacking force.

BERLIN

The capital of the *Reich* was a formidable target. In 1943 it was the third largest city in the world with over four million inhabitants and an urban area of over 1,500 square kilometres. Its enormous size filled the entire screen of an H2S radar, making it difficult to identify targets. It was home to large weapons production centres such as the *Alkett* and *Borsigwerke* factories and many others of strategic importance, such as *Zeiss* or *AEG*.

Most of Berlin comprised solid, five or six storey buildings on either side of broad streets, which reduced the effectiveness of incendiary bombs. Most of the buildings had reinforced basements, the city had a major Metro system, and a large number of air raid shelters had been built. Its anti-aircraft defences were impressive and growing all the time.

Several ways of reducing the number of losses were tried, such as launching diversionary attacks, using rudimentary electronic countermeasures and systems to jam German fighters' communications systems, improving target illumination systems, and reducing the time spent over the target. None was particularly effective.

On 22 November, what would prove to be the worst attack on the centre of Berlin was launched. Seven hundred aircraft dropped 2,500 tons of bombs with

Despite his difficult temperament and the complicated relationship he had with both his subordinates and superiors, Harris had a sincere concern for the welfare and survival of his men. But few dared to contradict him.

A BOMB AIMER'S EXPERIENCE

"Lying in the nose of a Lancaster on a visual bomb run over Berlin was probably the most frightening experience of my life time. Approaching the target, the city appeared to be surrounded by rings of searchlights, and the flak was always intense. The run-up seemed endless, the minutes of flying 'straight and level' seemed like hours and every second I expected to be blown to pieces. I sweated with fear, and the perspiration seemed to freeze on my body."

Flight Lieutenant R.B. Leigh

reasonable accuracy through a thick bank of clouds. Around 2,000 were killed and another 180,000 were left homeless.

The Americans and the British continued to wage two different wars, despite what had been decided in inter-allied conferences and despite the priority given to the invasion. At no time did Harris seriously entertain the idea of supporting the Eighth Air Force in their campaign against more profitable targets or in bleeding the *Luftwaffe* dry. Until the end he would remain convinced that area bombing was the way to win the war, against all evidence to the contrary. And he would impose his conviction on others, in defiance of orders received and sometimes even being openly backed by Churchill who would flout the chain of command. Harris was giving the British people something they wanted, and he became an almost untouchable figure who could do no wrong. To all intents and purposes he was running his own ship.

HARRIS'S OPTIMISM

"From these calculations it appears that the Lancaster force alone should be sufficient, but only just sufficient, to produce in Germany by 1 April 1944 a state of devastation in which surrender is inevitable."

ANALYSIS

In the first nineteen days of the new offensive three attacks were launched on Berlin and five on other targets, with poor results and high losses. In that period Bomber Command lost a third of its four-engine bombers and a quarter of its aircrews. The principal cause was the night fighter. The *Stirling* received the worst punishment, followed by the *Halifax*.

The larger the attacking force, the higher the percentage of losses, due to the longer time they had to spend over the target, which gave the enemy fighters time to home in on the bombers. But to be able to drop a minimally effective tonnage of bombs it was necessary to fall back on the *Halifax* and *Stirling* bombers. It was a vicious circle which was hard to break.

THE DISASTER AT NÜREMBERG

A total of 795 aircraft attacked Nüremberg in April and only 700 returned, a loss rate of nearly 12 per cent. This was a totally unacceptable percentage, especially since accuracy over the target had been nil. One hundred and twenty aircraft attacked Schweinfurt by mistake and a good number of the others dropped their bombs onto the countryside. Harris himself admitted that this scale of losses was unacceptable: 545 fliers died (compared to 507 pilots during the *entire* Battle of Britain). It was the worst disaster suffered by Bomber Command in the war.

During the autumn and winter months the weather seemed to support Harris's views, since American raids lost much of their accuracy and only area bombing had any chance of causing any real damage. But, even so, the British knew that in summer there would be no more than ten nights with good enough visibility, a figure which would shrink by half in winter. Even though radar and navigational aids helped pinpoint the target, the return to bases shrouded in fog or lashed by rain was a recipe for a high accident rate as tired aircrews nursed damaged aircraft home.

Ideal conditions were when the weather was clear over Britain and foggy or with low cloud over Germany (making the enemy fighters' task more difficult), then over the target there should be some clear sky. This very rarely happened.

Throughout the conflict bombing accuracy would always be very limited. The desired concentration of bombs over the right target would never be achieved, whether by visual or radar bombing. To a certain extent all bombing was area bombing, since only a small percentage of the bombs would land within a certain distance

TACTICS

In order to reduce the number of aircraft lost it was decided to decrease the time aircraft spent over the target. From the sixteen aircraft a minute on missions in August, the rate was stepped up to thirty-four aircraft a minute by the end of the year (by 1944 the figure would be over forty). This meant mixing together all types of aircraft rather than separating aircraft types into waves according to their various performances. The most experienced crews would lead the wave and the newest would be at the rear. The *Stirlings*, flying at a lower altitude, were always afraid of being hit by bombs dropped from aircraft flying high above them. By the end of November 1943 *Stirlings* would cease to form part of the longer distance missions because their contribution in terms of tonnage of bombs was limited and their loss rate was prohibitive.

of a specific target. At night it was even
worse. Readings from the H2S radar were
tremendously unreliable while the more
accurate system, the *Oboe*, only reached
as far as the Ruhr. To make things worse,
methods of estimating the results of an attack
and the damage done were very imprecise
and the conclusions drawn more so.

Midway through 1943, in an
attempt to improve bombing
accuracy, Harris prohibited
bombers from taking evasive
action to avoid flak.

The *Luftwaffe* had developed effective
countermeasures against *Window*, such as
the *Würzlaus* and *Nürnberg* systems, and
had started to use the new SN-2 radar, which
was immune to *Window*. The *Naxos* system
could detect H2S signals from pathfinders
and the friend or foe identification systems
of the bombers. The production of anti-aircraft
cannons grew to a total of 8,400 heavy and nearly
51,000 light guns in 1944. All this, combined with the
need for people to operate them (an extra 250,000 men
and 110,000 women in 1944), diverted resources away from
other critical areas. But the flak defences were highly effective,
only limited by the scarcity of ammunition; in one attack on
Berlin in March 1944 nearly half a formation of B-17 *Flying Fortresses* were
damaged by anti-aircraft fire.

BOMBS

The most frequently used bombs were 250 and 500-pound high explosive devices, of
which nearly 20 per cent were duds that failed to explode on impact. The incendiary
bombs were mostly four-pound magnesium devices, dropped in containers designed
to scatter them over the target area. In a normal raid over half a million such bombs
might be dropped on one city. More dangerous were the 30-pound phosphorous
devices, which were used much less often.

The most spectacular were the 4,000-pound bombs (there was even an 8,000-pound
version), known as *Blockbusters* or *Cookies*. They basically consisted of cylinders filled
with explosive, with no penetration
capability but whose main effect, in
addition to occasionally demolishing a
building, was to destroy roofs and knock
out windows to enhance the effect
of the incendiary bombs and aid the
spread of fires. The first versions were
dropped with a parachute, prompting
the Germans to call them "aerial mines".

A TYPICAL MISSION

After all available geographic, economic and meteorological data had been painstakingly collected, a target was chosen. Then a great deal of hard work began at all levels. Precise instructions were issued to four or five bomber groups, setting out the size of the formation, the bomb payload, the courses to the target area, and the timetable, coordinated in such a way that all the bombs would be dropped in a maximum period of twenty minutes in order to maximize the effect.

Very specific orders were given regarding the use of communications, *Window*, and enemy radar jamming systems, and regarding the method to be used to mark the target (in general illumination flares and green and/or red markers in different shapes and patterns). The pathfinder and the master (lead) bomber (when one was designated as such) had to drop their markers over the target in around eleven minutes, after which the main force had to spot them and drop their bombs as close as possible.

Night flying was very demanding on the pilot, who often could not see the other aircraft. The absence of a co-pilot after 1942 meant that another crew member had to be capable of taking his place if necessary, but he would of course lack the training of the pilot. The cold was a constant for all the crew except for the radio-operator of a *Lancaster* who would be roasted since his station was just where the rudimentary heating ducts were. The crew members took all kinds of stimulants, including amphetamines, in order to stay alert during missions.

The main force might be spread over some thirty kilometres across a ten kilometre front, with a gap between the lowest and highest flying aircraft of around 1,500 metres. The formation would be quite open, flying low over British territory before climbing to 6-7,000 metres to reach their target and drop their bombs at maximum speed. Then they would start their journey home, at an altitude never less than 2,500 metres.

Despite occasional missions in support of the Eighth Air Force, Harris continued with his offensive against cities, returning to Berlin in February and March, although at a high price. The aircrews' morale was becoming seriously affected and many of them saw the end of their tour of thirty missions they needed to complete before getting a new posting as very far off indeed. One of the signs that morale was starting to suffer was the high number of aircraft that were turning back

Cologne in ruins after the raids.

early due to technical or other reasons. The lack of rest after several consecutive nights flying missions was one of the reasons behind this phenomenon, but Harris appeared not to see what was so obvious.

On 19 February there was another disaster, this time over Leipzig, when seventy-eight bombers were lost in exchange for minimal results. The weather forecast was hopelessly wrong and the aircraft encountered winds far weaker than they had expected, which caused the formation to break up as the navigators failed to compensate for them. The opposite occurred on 24 March when seventy-four aircraft were lost (out of 811) when they had to fight winds of over 200 kilometres an hour, causing aircraft to end up over 100 kilometres off course. The meteorologists were starting to learn about the jet stream.

The Nüremberg disaster in April finally brought an end to this type of mission in order to focus on supporting the invasion. Bomber Command was now under the nominal command of SHAEF (Supreme Headquarters Allied Expeditionary Force), in other words Eisenhower. Harris, although it pained him, had no option but to devote most of his resources to operations over France, in an attempt to destroy enemy communications systems prior to the imminent invasion.

Although some isolated missions were flown over targets in Germany, for several months the British concentrated on daytime missions over targets in France protected by a fighter escort; as a result accuracy increased and losses decreased significantly. The morale of the aircrews recovered since the results were much more obvious and chances of survival were much higher. Nevertheless there were still some disastrous missions, such as the one over Mailly-le-Camp during which 42 out of 346 aircraft were lost.

CAUSES OF THE FAILURE OVER BERLIN

In six months, 19 major raids were flown against Berlin, with a total of 10,813 missions and the loss of 625 aircraft (5.8 per cent) and 2,700 fliers. Of the aircraft that took off, 9,560 reached their target, dropping 33,390 tons of bombs (nearly half of them incendiary). Among the high explosive bombs were 6,811 4,000-pound devices and 53 8,000-pound bombs. Over five million 4-pound incendiary bombs were dropped. But the city survived and the morale of its inhabitants remained unbroken. Among the reasons behind the lack of any decisive results were:

- Insufficient bomb payloads at the right concentration when only *Lancasters* were used. *Halifax* bombers, which carried a higher percentage of incendiary bombs, were much more effective for destroying cities.
- Poor performance of the pathfinders in terms of finding and marking the target with a minimum degree of accuracy, unless the target could be identified visually.
- Loss of morale of the aircrews in a context of high casualty rates and dubious results, made worse by Bomber Command's insistence on repeatedly flying missions over the Reich's most feared and best defended target. This was reflected in a high rate of aborted missions and premature bomb-dropping regardless of the markers dropped by the pathfinders.

As from September 1944, Eisenhower ceased to have control over strategic bombing forces, although he retained the right to call for them if the need arose. This signalled the start of the most intensive period of bombing of the entire war, against the backdrop of a fierce internal debate over what was the best way to use Bomber Command. In the last eight months of the war the Allies dropped 75 per cent of the total number of bombs used in the entire conflict, accounting for the deaths of over half the number of civilians who were killed in bombing raids during the war.

A *Lancaster* flying at low altitude. It was the most manoeuvrable of all the allied four-engine bombers.

The Allies wanted to finish the war as soon as possible in order to minimize casualties and prevent Germany from developing a weapon that might turn the situation around (V weapons, chemical or biological weapons, or even nuclear ones). The pressure on land would be accompanied by a growing pressure from the air, which would not only destroy the economy but also, it was supposed, would speed up the advance of allied ground troops. In late 1944 Harris devoted a good deal of his resources (a quarter of the tonnage of bombs dropped) to the combined campaign against fuel production, but he never ceased to be sceptical about its effectiveness nor did he stop advocating indiscriminate and unlimited area bombing.

To the end Harris concentrated on his personal crusade to wipe out German cities, although he continued to occasionally divert resources to attack synthetic fuel facilities on the Ruhr. His targets were now small cities which up to now had been spared. Although

Recreation of a briefing. The Wing Commander and the Meteorological Officer reporting on conditions over Berlin.

BATTLE FATIGUE

At any moment there was the constant threat of attack by night fighters, collision with other bombers or, over the target, being hit by bombs dropped by overflying aircraft. The tension was enormous and many crew members were unable to withstand it, creating a serious medical, administrative and disciplinary problem which was never properly addressed and certainly not resolved in Britain. Once back at base there was a debriefing session and then a well-earned rest.

In the RAF anxiety caused by the stress of battle tended to be classified as "*lack of moral fibre*" (LMF), a terrible stigma for those suffering from it. Cases of real cowardice were very scarce but authentic cases of "*battle fatigue*" were on the increase. Between 1942 and 1945, 8,400 crew members were assessed by psychiatrists who diagnosed a thousand of them with "*lack of moral fibre*". A third of them were pilots. This percentage is low considering the low survival rate: one out of four would survive one tour of duty and one out of ten survived two tours.

some contained communications nodes or military industries, most of the targets were simply urban areas. He launched a number of daylight attacks, enjoying conditions of total air superiority (as secured by the Eighth Air Force with the entry into service of the long-range escort fighter, the P51 *Mustang*).

Although Harris was coming under scrutiny from both his superiors and the government, he was enormously popular among the aircrews and the British people and he still had considerable influence over Churchill. To replace him now would not only be a blow to morale but there was also a very real risk that the Americans would take control of Bomber Command and place one of their men at its head. This was something that the British simply could not allow.

The *Luftwaffe* continued to be a very dangerous enemy and missions could still be more costly than was either expected or acceptable, although the battle of attrition had for some time been going the Allies' way. Bomber Command's losses fell from an average of 7 per cent in the summer to 1.5 per cent in the last months of the war. The average life of a *Lancaster* in 1943 was twenty-two missions, a figure which had increased to sixty by 1945. The German night fighter force was depleted and the aircrews lacked the resources to maintain a minimum standard. Technologically the Ju 88G was very dangerous with its arsenal of *Naxos* and *Monica* detectors and SN-2 radar, but the Allies were developing effective countermeasures.

The last months of the war would see some of the most devastating attacks, such as the raids on Berlin, Chemnitz and Dresden in east Germany. All of these cities were full of refugees and it was clear that the civilian death toll would be very high.

After the Dresden bloodbath, Churchill had another change of mind and began openly to distance himself from Harris. Public opinion began to question this type of raids with victory being so close and elections around the corner. The United States was increasingly more critical, even with its traditional Anglo-Saxon double standard. But Harris continued with his labour of destruction. Seven hundred *Lancasters* razed the ruins of Cologne on 2 March, just four days before American troops entered the city. A week later 1,000 bombers dropped 4,600 tons of bombs on what remained of Essen, a few hours before the arrival of the American troops. On 14 April it was Potsdam's turn...

1. Loading a 2,000-pound bomb into a *Mosquito*.

2. In 1945 there were over 1,000 operational *Lancasters*.

Churchill rebuked Portal over the continuation of this campaign of senseless destruction; Portal replied that he had already ordered Harris to cease these attacks. At that time the Eighth Air Force was only carrying out purely tactical raids, already thinking ahead to its future offensive against Japan.

In the final months of the war, now at the zenith of its power, Bomber Command could field over 1,600 bombers, over 1,000 of them *Lancasters*. The consumption of resources was huge. A four-engine bomber equipped with *Gee*, H2S, and other electronic devices was extremely expensive and it is estimated that *Lancaster* production accounted for half the available budget. In 1945 Harris ordered over 67,000 missions and lost 600 aircraft. The campaign of destruction lasted to the very end. By late January Germany was nearly paralyzed as a result of the destruction of its railways, its synthetic fuel production plants, and its water and gas pipelines. But that did not prevent Harris from continuing with the systematic destruction of the few urban areas still standing almost up to the end of the war. Whether this had any moral or military justification is quite another story.

DRESDEN

Pressure from Stalin, who wanted his troops to attack an enemy with its rearguard destroyed, uncertainty regarding the *Reich's* capabilities of staging a last-ditch defence at a hypothetical "national redoubt", and Harris's obsession with total destruction, all combined in the decision to launch a devastating attack on the beautiful city of Dresden on the night of 13-14 February. It was a city thronging with refugees which could scarcely be considered a military target .

796 *Lancasters* attacked in two waves and dropped 2,646 tons of bombs (1,181 of which were incendiary devices) on the city centre (which was almost undefended), immediately creating numerous small fires which soon raged out of control.

The weather conditions combined to produce the third firestorm of the war and in a few hours some 40,000 people died (the exact figure still remains the subject of debate). Twenty-five square kilometres of the city was destroyed. On the following day the Eighth Air Force launched two more attacks. Theoretically the target was the city's railway yards but poor visibility due to the fires meant that they attacked urban areas instead. In total, over 4,000 tons of bombs fell on Dresden in twenty-four hours.

6

Appraisal

The first premise when passing judgement on the bombing campaign is to situate it in its historical context. When Japan attacked Pearl Harbor few Americans would object to the indiscriminate bombing of Japanese cities. Few Spaniards would criticize the taking of brutal reprisals after the massacre at Monte Arruit in the Rif War. The case was the same with the British during the Battle of Britain. The effectiveness of the bombing campaign has been repeatedly called into question and there is certainly objective data to suggest that its strategic effectiveness was below expectations, while it consumed a massive and disproportionate amount of resources.

The morality of the campaign is also seriously questioned; it inflicted an enormous amount of suffering on the German civilian population which probably contributed very little to the final allied victory.

But there are also reasons for defending the strategy. Firstly, Bomber Command's night campaign cannot be considered separately from the Eighth Air Force's daytime

1. The entire range of bombs carried by British bombers.

2. The De Havilland Mosquito became one of the most versatile aircraft of the war.

3. The Distinguished Flying Cross, a frequently awarded medal.

4. The aircrew of a shot down four-engine bomber had a 20 per cent probability of survival.

campaign, even though their tactics and targets were so different. And it was the daytime campaign which was to prove decisive in securing supremacy in the skies over Europe as an essential step prior to the invasion.

In addition to devastating civilian targets, British area bombing also caused considerable damage to German industry and infrastructure, making an essential contribution to the advance of land troops inland from Normandy. But it did not crush the morale of the German people, nor did it appreciably reduce industrial output, and in itself the campaign did not even wear down the *Luftwaffe*.

Unlike daylight bombing, the effectiveness of night area bombing depended on the absence of opposition. If they were lucky, bombers could shoot down an enemy fighter or two but under normal circumstances it was the other way round. In that respect the

bombing campaign had contributed virtually nothing to *Luftwaffe* attrition, although it did, of course, oblige the Germans to use considerable resources which otherwise could have been used in other theatres where their presence might have been decisive.

But the fact is that, with the resources available to the allied bombers in 1940, the results were as good as could be expected. Intelligence services provided very limited and often erroneous information regarding the strategic targets considered to be important. Accuracy was very poor, especially at night, so it was useless trying to concentrate bombing on any target smaller than a city centre, since the likelihood of most of the bombs hitting a smaller target was remote. Not even the technologically advanced *Norden* bombsights used in ideal daytime conditions could guarantee the accuracy required to hit important targets while respecting the civilian population. The main problem with night bombing, which remained unresolved throughout the war, was the lack of any adequate way of accurately marking the target. All the other shortcomings and limitations merely aggravated this basic problem and further reduced effectiveness.

And in order to obtain significant results from a bombing campaign it was necessary to repeatedly deliver a massive bombing effort against the same target, day and night, something which up until autumn 1944 the *Luftwaffe* was able to prevent. After that autumn raids were carried out with minimal uncoordinated opposition, and in some cases, like Dresden, the results were without a doubt totally disproportionate and futile.

The effect of area bombing.

Notwithstanding the above, there can be no doubt that area bombing did have a certain impact on the German war effort. Repairs to the damage inflicted meant diverting resources needed in other theatres, and industrial output was partially and temporarily affected on many occasions, but on a scale far from that hoped for by the Allies. At most 1 per cent of the German workforce died as a result of

A HIGH PRICE

The production of heavy bombers accounted for nearly a third of British industrial production during the war. In 1944 industrial investment and national prestige weighed too heavily on the top brass to allow them to alter the bombing campaign. As early as April 1942 the US air attaché in London reported to Washington that, *"The British public have an erroneous belief, which has been fostered by effective RAF publicity, that the German war machine can be destroyed and the nation defeated by intensive bombing."*

The price paid by the aircrews of the British bombers was extremely high: of the 125,000 men who served in Bomber Command, 55,500 were killed, 8,400 wounded, and a further 10,000 taken prisoner.

the entire bombing campaign, both by day and by night. The absenteeism due to bombing (especially daylight bombing) was less than 5 per cent.

The greatest effect was without a doubt that of diverting fighter planes and anti-aircraft artillery and men from other theatres, thereby depriving the *Wehrmacht* of a fundamental component of their strategy. Thus in early 1943 nearly 60 per cent of all German fighter aircraft were occupied in the defence of the *Reich*. By October 1944 the figure had climbed to 80 per cent. The same could be said of the anti-aircraft batteries. In 1944 anti-aircraft defences required the manufacture of 4,000 guns a month and accounted for 20 per cent of all the ammunition produced, half the production of electronic goods, and a third of all optical devices. Nearly 900,000 soldiers manned the anti-aircraft defences.

It is highly debatable whether there was any moral justification for the bombing. There can be no question that the destruction of German cities was undeniably a terror campaign, but we should not forget that the Second World War was a total war. At that time, contrary to what people might think today, there was no doubt whatsoever that the very survival of the nations, peoples and societies involved was at stake.

What Chamberlain refused to see in 1938, Churchill had seen very clearly in 1940. With the *Wehrmacht* in full spate and the European continent lost, the future of the British Isles seemed uncertain to say the least and it was essential to maintain the morale of the people. Since a military return to the continent was a pipe dream at that time, the only way of counterattacking available to the United Kingdom was to launch a bombing offensive against the *Reich*. And given the limited resources available at the time, the only realistic targets were German cities.

Initially the bombing offensive was the way Churchill refused to accept what in 1940 appeared to be the most logical outcome of the war; victory by Germany. To attack in any manner and with any method within his power was to refuse to accept the evidence.

Then there is the traditional Anglo-Saxon double standard. The decision to launch an indiscriminate offensive against Germany was actually taken long before the *Luftwaffe* began its attacks on British cities. The intention was always

Bomber Command badge.

The bomber aircrews finally received their recognition: the Bomber Command Memorial.

to present Germany as the incarnation of evil, capable of the most barbaric acts, which justified any action taken against it, even before Germany had displayed any such evil. The problem is that the offensive continued after it was clear that it was not only senseless but also totally disproportionate and cruel.

Once victory was assured, doubts always arise over the legitimacy of actions which were not questioned when the situation was a matter of life or death. Once the war had been won, scapegoats were sought and Harris and especially the courageous aircrews of Bomber Command became the perfect candidates. They did their duty and paid a very high price, only to be unjustly condemned to oblivion and contempt after the war had been won.

MORAL ISSUES

From the comfort of our decadent post-war western societies it is easy to take a very critical standpoint, but in 1940 it was necessary to do something and not merely stand by while the world that had taken so much to build was destroyed, or trust in a hypothetical and impossible *status quo* with a determined and implacable enemy. The days when the only response from citizens was to observe a minute's silence and place flowers in memory of the victims was still a very long way off.

What can a society do when faced with a clear and immediate threat of being eradicated? Endure passively and stoically, trusting in the superiority of its cause and its values in the hope that the fire will burn itself out, while refusing to admit the very existence of the danger? Make more and more concessions to its enemies who, from an ever more advantageous position, will make increasingly more demands

until they achieve their ultimate goal? Or instead counterattack with whatever resources it has available, whether fair or unfair, proportionate or disproportionate, so that the conflict will not be one-sided and the enemy will discover that wars are two-way streets and that at any moment they may cease to be the oppressor to become the victim.

PART TWO

Storm Over Europe: The USAAF

7

The Birth of an Air Force

1. The first American heavy bomber from the 1920s.

2. The US Seversky P-35 fighter was one of the first aircraft to be built entirely of metal.

At the start of the Second World War the United States had a tiny air force (the twentieth largest in the world) compared to the major European powers, even though some politicians, among them President Roosevelt himself, were convinced that air power could be a determining factor in this conflict. In fact, in 1939 only around 2,000 aircraft of all types were manufactured. The invasion of France in May 1940 gave rise to a radical change; Roosevelt asked Congress for 50,000 aircraft a year.

The head of the *Army Air Corps*, Henry Arnold, soon found himself with 1,500 million dollars with which to build an air force. The Secretary of War, Stimson, appointed Robert Lovett (a former Navy pilot and prestigious New York lawyer) as his assistant for everything pertaining to the air force (*Assistant Secretary of War for Air*). Lovett would be the ideal person to organize an effective working group and handle such an awkward personality as Arnold.

HENRY HAP ARNOLD

He was born in 1886 into a family of German descent. A mediocre West Point graduate, he joined the recently created Aeronautical Division in 1911, when flying was a highly dangerous art. Of the first twenty-eight American military pilots, ten died in air accidents. Arnold was nearly killed in an accident in 1912 and swore never to fly again, but four years later he broke his vow. After the war he was stationed at San Diego where he had Spaatz and Eaker, two future figureheads of American aviation, under him.

On the desk in his office stood a carved plaque which said: "*The difficult we do today; the impossible takes a little longer.*" Very diplomatic towards his superiors, he remained aloof from his underlings, with whom he could be scathing. He suffered five heart attacks, the last of which would prove fatal.

One of his first decisions was to make the air force independent, and so in June 1941 the *US Army Air Corps* (USAAC) became the *US Army Air Forces* (USAAF), commanded by Arnold. From having 1,200 warplanes and 22,700 men in 1938, by December 1941 the air force could field 3,000 aircraft and 340,000 men. By 1944 American industry would have produced

The P-40 Warhawk was sturdy, fast and very well armed, but its range was short.

over 80,000 aircraft and the USAAF would have nearly 2.5 million personnel, a third of them servicemen and women. In March 1944 alone 9,000 aircraft were built, something which had been considered impossible three years previously. Confidence in air power was so great that it was thought that if the unlimited air offensive was successful, no ground offensive would be necessary.

AMERICAN STRATEGY IN 1941

In 1941 the Staff of the recently created air force produced Air War Planning Document AWPD-1 setting out the guidelines which were to govern American air strategy during the war:

1.- Support the defensive strategy in the Pacific in the initial phases of the war
2.- Start an unlimited strategic offensive against Germany as soon as possible
3.- Prepare an invasion of the continent
4.- Prepare an invasion of Japan through an unlimited offensive against Japanese metropolitan areas.

In May 1940 Arnold sent Spaatz to London, officially as an assistant military attaché, although his real mission was to study the way in which the British conducted air warfare. The UK had started its air offensive very early on in the war, although in a rather haphazard manner. Initially targets had been tactical, supporting the Royal Navy by attacking German surface vessels and naval bases.

DOUHET'S DOCTRINE

The Italian general Giulio Douhet believed that future wars would be short but extremely violent due to the massive use of aircraft to massacre the civil population in order to destroy the enemy's fighting spirit. In 1921, in his reference work entitled "*The Command of the Air*", he claimed that "*...It is not enough to shoot down all the birds in flight if you want to wipe out a species; there remain the eggs and the nest. Any distinction between belligerents and non-belligerents is no longer admissible today....because when nations are at war, everyone takes part in it: the soldier carrying his gun, the woman loading shells in a factory, the farmer growing wheat, the scientist experimenting in his laboratory...*" His theories would have a great influence on Allied strategists during the Second World War.

THE FIRST AIRCRAFT

The United States entered the war very poorly prepared for air warfare. Its principal heavy bomber was the B-18 *Bolo* and its fighter force consisted mainly of Curtiss P-40 *Warhawks* and a certain number of already obsolescent Seversky P-35s and Curtiss P-36 *Hawks*. The *Warhawk* was a development of the *Hawk* and served honourably throughout the war in various Allied air forces. Very fast at medium and low levels, it lacked power at high altitude and was less agile in dogfights than many of its enemies. Nevertheless, it was sturdy, reliable and very well armed with six 12.7mm (.50 calibre) machine guns. It was used by a total of fifteen USAAF fighter groups.

The Douglas B-18 *Bolo* was the bomber most used overseas at the start of the Second World War. Initially preferred to the YB-17, thirty-five units were acquired in two versions as a replacement for the limited Martin B-10. Many units were lost at Pearl Harbor and the *Bolo* was soon replaced by the much more capable B-17. It had a maximum speed of 350 km/h, a range of 1,900 kilometres, and could carry up to three tons of bombs. For defensive armament it was fitted with three 7.62mm machine guns.

Later the RAF launched a half-hearted campaign against German cities based on daylight bombing, which proved to be tremendously costly when bombers came up against the powerful *Luftwaffe*.

Only the introduction of heavy bombers, such as the *Stirling*, the *Halifax* and, in particular, the *Lancaster*, enabled the Allies to start their night offensive against major civilian targets, an offensive which would be maintained until the end of the war.

The creation of the Eighth Air Force in January 1942 signalled the start of the implementation of the Allied strategy formulated in the Arcadia Conference (December 1941-January 1942), which consisted of first defeating Germany before later concentrating on Japan. Arnold appointed Spaatz as his commander and Eaker as head of Eighth Bomber Command. At the same time he chose a number of civilians to manage the enormous structure he was about to create. One of his ideas

The first Boeing B-17 aircraft to be delivered caused quite a stir.

ORGANIZATION

The Eighth Air Force was initially divided into four commands: Bomber, Fighter, Ground Support, and Logistics. Bomber Command was divided into several wings, each consisting of three groups of four squadrons of around twelve aircraft each. Later, several wings (from three to five) would be grouped into air divisions. For the purpose of air control, each squadron was split into flights of six aircraft and sections of three.

was that: "*You can take a smart executive and make a fair Army officer out of him in a few months. You can never take a dumb Army officer and make a good combat leader out of him.*"

The weapon that made the creation of this bombing force possible was the Boeing B-17. This innovative machine had been developed in the 1930s and entered into service in 1937. The aircraft, built entirely of metal, was fitted with four 750 HP radial engines which made it faster than any American fighter at that time. It could carry two tons of bombs a distance of 1,300 kilometres and drop them from a height of 8,000 metres. It had a formidable defensive armament of as many as thirteen 12.7mm machine guns, which in theory made it a difficult target for the fighters of the day.

The capabilities of this new aircraft, dubbed the *Flying Fortress*, were such that initially it was thought that it would need no fighter escort, an idea which would cost many aircrews dearly. Billy Mitchell, of whom more later, had preached that a balanced air force (whose objective was the destruction of the enemy's air force in order to then be able to destroy their economy), should consist of at least 60 per cent fighter aircraft. Air superiority was essential for the success of an air offensive but the American leaders would take over a year to take this on board, blinded by the enormous possibilities of the B-17.

An early version of the B-17.

A *Flying Fortress* assembly line.

Initially the British wanted the Americans to hand a large number of aircraft over to them, especially bombers, to be operated under British control on night missions. This ran totally counter to American strategic thinking, which was based on a belief that precision daylight bombing of strategic targets was a much more effective way to win the war than indiscriminately bombing civilian targets during the night.

1. A trainee pilot with his trainer plane.

2. Henry Hap Arnold.

Arnold charged Eaker with the task of negotiating with the British the procurement of everything he needed to create the huge infrastructure in England that his bombers would need: airfields, roads, accommodation, etc. Eaker had no experience of bombers but he had flown fighter planes. Arnold aimed to instil his bomber crews with an aggressive spirit, one more typical of a fighter force.

On 21 February 1942, Eaker arrived in London and, three days later, he moved to High Wycombe, setting up his headquarters just eight kilometres away from British Bomber Command's HQ.

IRA EAKER

Ira was born in Texas in 1896. He was a short, stocky, rough-looking man, and an insatiable reader, who knew how to convince men with his words and his gentlemanly manner.

He made the first all-instrument intercontinental flight. Among his pre-war postings he served on the aircraft carrier *Lexington*. In January 1942 he was entrusted with the organization of Eighth Air Force bomber units. He knew the British very well and was the ideal person to work with them, in the midst of the doctrinal differences between the two nations.

In December 1942 he took command of the Eighth Air Force and would go on to become the commander of all US air forces in Great Britain. Later he would command the air forces in the Mediterranean theatre. He would rack up 12,000 flying hours over thirty years. He died in 1987.

3. Refuelling a B-17.

4. The mechanics were the unsung heroes of the Eighth Air Force.

Initially there was massive disagreement with the British. Harris, who had just taken command of Bomber Command, was convinced of the impossibility of a daylight offensive. In fact, they had used some B-17s on daylight missions using very few aircraft with poor results. But Arnold intended to use them in large compact formations so as to take advantage of their great firepower which he believed would allow them to defend one another from attack. In a tense dinner with Arnold, Eaker, Harris and Portal (then Chief of Staff of Bomber Command) at the table, Eaker suggested a strategy which was eventually agreed upon and would last until the end of the war: the British would bomb by night and the Americans by day, without giving the German defences any respite.

Strangely enough, and despite their different personalities, relations between Harris and Eaker would be very cordial throughout the war. Eaker refrained from giving voice to his ideas that the bombing of civilians was not only immoral but pointless, while Harris was committed to killing a large number of skilled workers who would not be easy to replace, and their families, in order to undermine German morale. Before the war the Americans had already developed a doctrine which established "legitimate" targets based on a study of the American industrial fabric. According to this doctrine, modern economies were based on "bottlenecks" such as steel, bearings, and electricity production,

plus rail transport. It was therefore not necessary to annihilate the civil population; all that was required was to destroy structures that were critical for industry. The economy would collapse and with it the will to fight.

BOMBER COMMAND'S NIGHT BOMBING

The British doctrine was based on the night bombing of civilian targets in order to kill as many skilled workers as possible and their families too, so as to undermine the morale of the civilian population. Any target was therefore legitimate, regardless of the civilian casualties caused, and regardless of whether they were women, children, the sick or the elderly. Churchill found in Harris the perfect exponent of this doctrine, one which the Americans found not only ineffective, but also abhorrent and immoral.

Bomber Command had three basic types of bombers for this mission, the Short *Stirling*, the Handley Page *Halifax*, and the Avro *Lancaster*. The latter would bear by far the greatest burden of the British operations. The *Lancaster* had an empty weight of around 16 tons, an aircrew of seven men, and was powered by four Rolls-Royce or Packard Merlin engines, each developing 1,460 HP. Maximum speed was 445 km/h although cruise speed was around 320 km/h at an altitude of 4,500 metres. The service ceiling was 6,700 metres and the maximum range in the region of 4,000 kilometres. The bombload varied greatly depending on the mission but it was the only aircraft capable of carrying Grand Slam bombs weighing nearly ten tons. Its defensive armament consisted of eight 7.7mm machine guns in two twin turrets and one quadruple turret. Nearly 7,400 aircraft of various versions would be built between October 1941 and October 1945.

The night terror offensive was very controversial during the war and continues to be so now. It is very likely that its contribution to Germany's defeat was minimal, especially if we compare it with the American offensive. It did draw a good deal of resources from other theatres and it certainly terrorized the civil population, but the massacres the offensive caused can have no justification, either from a moral, economic, or military standpoint. And the price paid was terrible; of the 125,000 aircrew who served in Bomber Command, 55,500 died, 8,400 were wounded, and nearly 10,000 became prisoners of war.

An aircrew before a mission.

Belief in daylight precision bombing of specific targets, made possible by technological advances, fitted in perfectly with the American mentality which found the prospect of indiscriminately murdering women and children appalling, at least in Europe. It was a concept that was radically opposed to Harris's ideas, but Arnold was able to uphold it despite pressure from the British.

Harris initially "lent" Arnold five airfields in East Anglia and soon the construction of another sixty was under way. It would not be an easy task. England was rather short on manpower and bringing men over from the other side of the Atlantic would take time. The construction of the three runways that a typical airfield required cost some 500,000 pounds (in the money of the time) and the associated buildings and structures the same amount again. Despite this, the rate of construction was extraordinary, even by today's standards. In June 1943, 13,500 Americans and 32,000 British were building airfields in the south of England.

There began an incessant and gradually increasing flow of convoys carrying American personnel to the British Isles. Initially the British welcomed the Americans enthusiastically, since they thought it was about time that their Allies turned up to fight alongside them after three years struggling against Hitler alone. But very soon the different mentalities of the two peoples would start to clash, giving rise to incidents that were sometimes funny but others not so amusing. The locals were often happy to invite the young Americans into their homes to spend a weekend or to have dinner together. But there were also times when the American guests stepped over the line, even to the point of sexual assault, although such episodes were exceptional.

The United States brought all kinds of equipment to the UK to keep their units operational.

WILLIAM "BILLY" MITCHELL

The son of a senator, he served in the Hispano-American War and had a liking for wearing tall riding boots and smart uniforms. He was the first American to arrive at the Western Front in the Great War and the first to fly over enemy lines. Towards the end of the war he succeeded Pershing, the commander of the American expeditionary force, and launched a great air offensive during the campaigns of St Mihiel and the Argonne. He had the same ideas as his British counterpart Trenchard, who was determined to create a strategic bomber force in order to respond to German attacks on London.

A great defender of air power, off his own bat he developed a comprehensive theory regarding the ability of strategic aviation to win wars. After the experience of the Western Front, he thought that a strategic air offensive could save the lives of many front line soldiers by destroying the enemy's industrial capabilities and breaking the morale of its people, so rendering it incapable of continuing the war, which would be brought to an end in a handful of weeks. In one of the scenarios that he proposed, the city of New York was bombed using asphyxiating gases. The population was evacuated but with the survivors unable to rebuild their lives, the government was forced to capitulate.

Together with Douhet he refuted Clausewitz's classical doctrine. While for Clausewitz the objective of war was to destroy the enemy's armed forces, for Mitchell and Douhet air power would prevent armies from engaging by destroying the enemy's political and economic centres from the air.

AIR POWER

Another of Mitchell's revolutionary ideas was that air power could destroy an enemy fleet, which flew in the face of the doctrine that prevailed in 1921. A year later, six 1,000 kilo bombs sank the old German battleship *Ostfriesland* in a demonstration organized by Mitchell. Although Mitchell met with strong criticism from the government, when he died in 1936 he left behind him some faithful followers such as Arnold, Eaker and Spaatz.

On 1 July 1942 a B-17 with an American aircrew landed on British soil, the first of many. That same month a number of aircrews of the Eighth Air Force went to England to train on British aircraft during low-level raids on the *Reich*. On the 4th they attacked airfields in Holland using Douglas A-20 medium bombers. On 17 August there was a raid involving a handful of aircraft on a railway station near Rouen in occupied France, with an escort of British *Spitfires*. In command was Paul Tibbets, who would later become famous for dropping the first atom bomb on Japan. Bombing from high altitude in daylight, only one aircraft suffered slight damage from anti-aircraft fire. This was a very promising start which seemed to support American thinking against the British doctrine.

The young American pilots soon won the hearts of British women.

The escort fighters scarcely had enough range to accompany the bombers at that time. In August there were only four American fighter groups in Great Britain, two of them equipped with P-38 *Lightnings* and the other two with British *Spitfires*.

The range of the *Spitfire* was too short for them to act as fighter escorts.

But in the same month of July there was a meeting between Churchill and Roosevelt at the White House that significantly upset Arnold's plans. The falls of Tobruk and Crimea and the aggressive U-boat offensive seemed to herald a new and unstoppable German push. Churchill wanted to create a second front as soon as possible at whatever the cost and he used all his not inconsiderable negotiating skills to put pressure on the Americans. He believed it vital to raise the morale of the British people at a critical time and only the Americans were in a position to do so. The only feasible way to counter-attack in the short term consisted of an invasion of North Africa, the future "Operation Torch". But this meant diverting part of the incipient Eighth Air Force to the Mediterranean theatre. Two recently arrived groups, the 97th and the 301st, would be transferred in early autumn, while other groups in training in America would be sent directly to the new theatre of operations.

CROSSING THE ATLANTIC: FROM THE UNITED STATES TO ENGLAND

Moving the *Flying Fortresses* to their British bases in East Anglia would be a highly complicated and risky business. The pilots had little experience and yet they had to cross the Atlantic in winter following a route that was no walk in the park. From Maine they had a first leg of 700 miles to Labrador or Terranova. From there they flew between 800 and 1,000 miles to one of the two bases recently built in Greenland. Landing at those bases required great skill and a cool head and not all the pilots were successful. There then remained two more legs, the first to Ireland and from there finally to the UK, where on many days visibility was minimal due to fog and rain.

A British truck on an airfield.

The original plan of having a thousand operational bombers by April 1943 to make mass attacks on the *Reich* was postponed *sine die*.

One added risk of this situation was that the Eighth Air Force, now even more embryonic, was at a greater risk of being absorbed by the RAF for night raids, which would mean its virtual disappearance. In order to prevent this from happening, Arnold thought that his only chance lay in immediately demonstrating the effectiveness of daylight bombing raids, even at the risk of having to use small formations manned by aircrews with little training. But time was pressing and before autumn ("Operation Torch" was planned for November) he had to prove that his way of thinking was the way to go.

Hap Arnold with other officers of the Eighth Air Force.

Arnold pressured Eaker and Spaatz to start operations immediately and they were aware the future of the Eighth Air Force depended on the next ten to twelve missions. Arnold admitted: "*We didn't know how we were going to make the offensive work. We just knew that we had to make it work.*" Eaker and Spaatz had faith in their airmen, in their aircraft and, most especially, in the doctrine of precision daylight strategic bombing. Late in the summer of 1942 a small group of young Americans, operating out of British airfields, were going to try and demonstrate something in which very few believed.

A Mitchell B-25 medium bomber.

8

First Missions, First Disappointments

Throughout the months of September and October the Eighth Air Force began to carry out increasingly more ambitious missions against close targets in occupied continental territory. On many occasions, as far as their range allowed, they were temporarily escorted by RAF *Spitfires*.

German opposition was increasingly heavier and on 9 October, on a mission over Lille and St. Omer in the north of France, four Fortresses failed to return and forty-six more were damaged to a greater or lesser extent. The result was very poor, not only because of the aircraft loss and battle damage figures, but also because the gunners on board the bombers had shown serious signs of inexperience. Firing wildly they had hit their own planes; bombers and escort fighters alike. On reaching home they claimed 102 German fighters shot down, many more than the *Luftwaffe* had actually put up (in fact the Germans lost just two aircraft).

It was thought that the B-17s would be able to penetrate anti-aircraft defences by flying at a high altitude, defend themselves from fighters with their powerful armament, and carry out daylight precision bombing.

6 SEPTEMBER: FIRST LOSSES

After bombing an aircraft factory in the north of France on 6 September, the B-17s were attacked by a large number of fighters, mostly Me 109s. Two of the *Flying Fortresses* were hit by cannon fire, exploded, and their remains fell to the ground in flames. Other aircraft were seriously damaged, among them the one flown by Tibbets. The cockpit was hit and the co-pilot lost a hand. Colonel Longfellow, later to command the Second Wing, a man with a well-deserved reputation for being very hard on his subordinates, was on board the aircraft as an observer and he threw himself at the controls, nearly putting the aircraft into a nosedive. Tibbets managed to regain control and flew the aircraft safely home.

These were the first two losses of the Eighth Air Force and a foretaste of what was to come.

Bombing accuracy had left much to be desired. The bomb-aimers had no combat experience with the Norden bombsights and found it difficult to enter the exact data in the midst of anti-aircraft fire and the stress of battle. Many pilots took evasive action to avoid anti-aircraft fire and, on some occasions, the bombers forgot to open the bomb bay doors. The navigators also made many mistakes, resulting in a circular error probable (CEP) of over a kilometre.

Nevertheless, Eaker considered Lille as the final proof that daylight bombing without a fighter escort was possible. The press did much to help foster this idea, so that although the actual results of the attack were more than questionable, the effect on morale was considerable.

However, the future of the Eighth Air Force now hung by a thread, since the North African invasion was imminent and, with it, the creation of a new air force, the Twelfth, which would be nicknamed "Junior". The popular

A B-24 *Liberator*: more were built than the B-17 and they had a larger payload, but they lacked the B-17s' glamour.

General Jimmy Doolittle, hero of the Tokyo air raid, was chosen to lead it, a man who originally had been earmarked to command the bomber groups of the Eighth Air Force. His men were drawn from the aircrews of the Eighth Air Force, which had temporarily been turned into an embryonic skeleton of what it would later become. The two most veteran groups, the 97th and the 301st, plus all the fighter groups, with the exception of the 4th, were transferred to the "Junior" force, a total of 27,000 men and nearly 1,200 aircraft up until November. Spaatz feared that if the Allies took North Africa, the Eighth Air Force, or what was left of it, would be disbanded and distributed along the Mediterranean coast.

But Eisenhower, already thinking about the future and the still far off invasion, had other plans, and it would be Spaatz who would take command of air operations in the Mediterranean, while Eaker would replace him as commander of the Eighth Air Force. The command of the bomber groups would be given to Longfellow.

A B-17 on an airfield in southern England.

The Eighth Air Force now faced a task that would be much tougher than had been originally thought; to attack the German submarine bases on the French coast in support of the Allied convoys sailing to North Africa. Up until then the Eighth Air Force's missions had consisted of raids on industrial targets in Holland and France, within escort fighter range, in order to minimize losses and demonstrate the viability of daylight precision bombing. Now, without a fighter escort, they had to attack targets that they were unable to destroy.

The Americans were aware that the big U-Boat pens were virtually indestructible, but they were confident of being able to damage enough of the port and neighbouring logistics facilities to hinder submarine operations. On 21 October, ninety bombers attacked Lorient with 900 kilogram bombs. Despite the accuracy of the bombing, the bunkers remained intact and forty French workers were killed. There was scarcely any flak since they were taken completely by surprise, but aggressive German fighters shot down three B-17s on the way home.

A type B-3 life vest.

COMPOSITION OF THE EIGHTH AIR FORCE IN NOVEMBER 1942

B-17 *Flying Fortress* groups: 91st, 303rd, 305th and 306th
B-24 *Liberator* groups: 44th and 93rd
Fighter groups: 4th

A *Flying Fortress* coming in to land.

THE AIRCREW OF A B-17

At the rear of the aircraft was the tail gunner, sitting in a claustrophobic space with twin machine guns that were belt fed from inside the fuselage. Further forward were the two waist gunners, each operating one machine gun, standing nearly back to back. A little further forward still was the ventral ball turret, which the gunner entered through a hatch that, once closed, left him totally isolated. He needed to be short and flexible since the turret had a diameter of just 90cm and he shared the space with two machine guns and their ammunition. There was no room for a parachute.

Up front, behind a door, was the radio room, the only closed off space in the aircraft. The radio operator had a small seat and a desk with radio equipment. He also operated a rear-facing machine gun fitted on the ceiling of the aircraft, firing through a large opening. In later, radar-equipped versions, the radar operator would sit in the same room.

Behind another bulkhead was the bomb bay, which could be crossed using a narrow, 35cm wide catwalk. After take-off the bombardier had to remove the safety pins from each bomb.

In front of the bomb bay was the mid-upper turret, just behind the flight deck. It was manned by an NCO who was also the flight engineer and mechanic. If he was not manning his guns he would sit behind the pilot, monitoring the engine gauges. The pilot sat on the left and the co-pilot on the right, both of them officers. They had around 150 dials and gauges to monitor. Below the

cockpit, a narrow opening led to the nose section where the other two officers, the navigator and the bombardier flew. The navigator sat at a small desk on the left. He had two side windows and an astrodome above him to determine the aircraft's position by the stars.

The bombardier's position was further forward in the most exposed place on the aircraft, behind the plexiglass nose. He had the use of one machine gun (in some versions there were two guns in lateral nose cheeks which were of very limited use). The bombardier used a Norden bombsight during the final bombing run, which allowed him to take control of the aircraft. The pilot handed over control to the bombardier and it was he who guided the aircraft in the final kilometres, trying to pinpoint the target accurately and to release the bombs at the right moment.

Despite the differences of rank and accommodation, relations between the crew members were closer than in the army. Most were volunteers who had recently been plucked from civilian life; few came from the regular army. The minimum rank was sergeant and all shared a very confined space during a mission. Formal discipline was very relaxed although everyone knew their place.

BOEING B-17 *FLYING FORTRESS*

1. Pilot and co-pilot seats

2. Mid-upper turret, operated by the flight engineer, with two 12.7mm guns

3. The radio operator's position, seen from behind, under the single 12.7mm upper dorsal gun

4. Crew entry hatch, in the left rear of the fuselage

5. The large tail fin was one of the design features that contributed towards the plane's magnificent manoeuvrability

6. Cockpit, bombardier's position, astrodome, and nose cheeks in the nose section

7. The remote control Bendix chin turret started to be installed in some F versions before becoming standard in the G version

8. Non-retractable ball turret with two 12.7mm guns

9. Waist gunner position. He was totally exposed to the cold

10. Tail turret for two 12.7mm guns and tail gunner's position

This innovative machine had been developed in the 1930s and entered into service in 1937. The aircraft, built entirely of metal, was fitted with four 750 HP radial engines which made it faster than any American fighter at that time. It could carry two tons of bombs a distance of 1,300 kilometres and drop them from a height of 8,000 metres. It had a formidable defensive armament, boasting as many as thirteen 12.7mm machine guns, which in theory made it a difficult target for the fighters of the day.

In the course of the war B-17s flew 295,000 missions over Europe, dropping 650,000 tons of bombs and losing a total of 4,483 aircraft in action and another 861 in accidents. Broken down by aircraft version, the numbers built were 512 version E, 3,400 version F, and 8,680 version G.

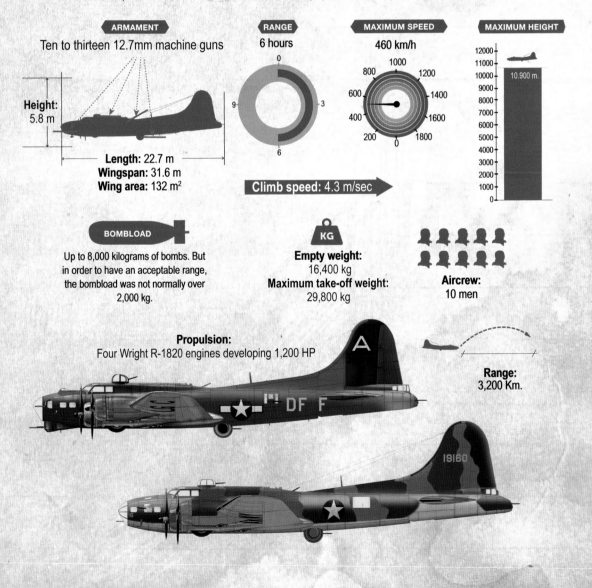

ARMAMENT
Ten to thirteen 12.7mm machine guns

Height: 5.8 m

Length: 22.7 m
Wingspan: 31.6 m
Wing area: 132 m^2

RANGE
6 hours

MAXIMUM SPEED
460 km/h

MAXIMUM HEIGHT
10.900 m.

Climb speed: 4.3 m/sec

BOMBLOAD
Up to 8,000 kilograms of bombs. But in order to have an acceptable range, the bombload was not normally over 2,000 kg.

KG
Empty weight:
16,400 kg
Maximum take-off weight:
29,800 kg

Aircrew:
10 men

Propulsion:
Four Wright R-1820 engines developing 1,200 HP

Range:
3,200 Km.

Bomb bay of a B-17.

The next target was St. Nazaire. By now the target was very well protected by heavy anti-aircraft defences and over half the bombers were damaged to some extent. Until the end of the year a further six missions would be flown against the submarine bases, without any appreciable damage being inflicted on any of them.

In addition to flak, the bombers' main enemy were German fighter aircraft. The German day fighter force was commanded by the young fighter ace Adolf Galland, who had two fighter wings (*Jagdgeschwader* or JG), JG2 and JG26, elite units manned by magnificent veteran pilots flying the latest model fighters. Their original armament nevertheless proved incapable of taking on the sturdy and well-protected American *Flying Fortresses*.

The *Luftwaffe's* fate was already sealed late in 1942 when the Chief of Staff, Jeschonnek, turned a deaf ear to Galland's plea to implement an urgent fighter construction programme in the face of the growing allied bombing offensive. Aircraft were also needed on the Eastern Front and in North Africa, causing fighters on the Western Front to continue to suffer from a low priority in *Luftwaffe* plans for far too long.

Despite their numerical disadvantage and limitations in terms of armament, the German pilots soon learned how to respond to the new threat. The traditional

CARL SPAATZ

Born into a family of German descent in 1891, Carl Andrew Spaatz graduated from West Point and immediately joined the newly formed Army Air Force. He shot down three aircraft during the First World War and ended the war as an excellent pilot. After being stationed as an observer during the Battle of Britain he was appointed assistant to the Chief of Air Corps, *General* Arnold. In July 1941 he was appointed Chief of Staff of the Air Force and, in May 1942, Commander of the Eighth Air Force, a position which he held concurrently with that of Commander-in-Chief of the USAAF in the European theatre.

He went on to take command of the strategic forces in Europe and led the bombing campaign. In 1945 he took command of the strategic forces in the Pacific and, after the war, took over from Arnold as Commanding General of the Army Air Forces. He was the first Chief of Staff of the new USAF in 1947. He died in 1974.

tactic of attacking singly from behind exposed fighters to a volume of defensive fire hitherto unknown (each bomber had some ten 12.7mm machine guns, six of them able to fire towards the rear). New tactics were required.

On 23 November the Fw 190s of JG2, led by Egon Meyer, surprised the Americans by attacking from the front, in groups of two or four aircraft. The bombers had very little defending guns aiming forward (just one or two machine guns) and Meyer took advantage of that weakness. The closing speed of the fighters was so high that they were in the defenders' sights for just seconds, while the effect of a number of 20mm cannons focusing their fire on the bombers' cockpit or engines from a mere hundred or so metres could be devastating.

One out of every three pilots and co-pilots of the 306th Group would be killed in such attacks in a few weeks.

Another of the bombers' greatest enemies was the weather. On only one out of every four missions was there good visibility over the target. Nearly half the missions scheduled would be called off; one out of ten of those called off due to adverse weather conditions would be with all the aircraft already in the air. Even when they could reach the target, the worst was often to come on the home journey. The changing weather in the south of England meant that a clear morning could become a thick bank of fog four or five hours later, which created a huge risk for returning aircraft, many of them with dead or wounded on board, with structural damage, or with one or two engines out of action.

"We'll bomb them by day. You bomb them by night. We'll hit them right around the clock" (Ira Eaker to Arthur Harris).

SPITFIRE

The first aircraft used to escort American bombers were the British *Spitfire* fighters which had performed so well as interceptors during the Battle of Britain. The *Spitfire* was agile, fast and had good firepower but its range was limited, which meant it could only stay with the bombers for a very short time, and only on missions in the north of France.

The initial version, armed with eight 7.7mm machine guns, had evolved a great deal. In the summer of 1942 the most common version was the Mk V, normally armed with four machine guns and two 20mm cannons. Powered by a Rolls-Royce Merlin engine developing 1,478 HP, its maximum speed was nearly 600 km/h at 6,000 metres. Its service ceiling was in the region of 11,000 metres and its range was around 600 kilometres.

MEDIUM BOMBERS

As well as big four-engine bombers the Eighth Air Force also used, albeit to a lesser extent, two types of medium bombers in the course of the campaign.

DOUGLAS A-20 HAVOC

In theory the A-20 replaced the A-17 but it was a completely different design with much better performance. It was one of the first warplanes with a nose wheel and was very pleasant to fly and highly manoeuvrable.

The first versions had poor defensive armament, which would later be upgraded. Although conceived as an attack aircraft, it was also used as a medium bomber.

It was the first aircraft to be used by the Eighth Air Force on a bombing raid over the continent, although it was soon replaced by other models. It would be extensively used by the RAF and the USAAF in various theatres.

ARMAMENT
Two 12.7mm machine guns in a mid-upper turret and a varying number in the nose, depending on the version. One 12.7mm gun mounted behind the bomb bay.

Height: 5.4 m

Length: 14.6 m
Wingspan: 18.7 m

Climb speed: 10.2 m/sec

RANGE
3.5 hours

MAXIMUM SPEED
546 km/h

MAXIMUM HEIGHT
7.200 m.

BOMBLOAD
Normally around 1,000 kg of bombs
(maximum 1,800 kg)

Technical specifications of the
DB-7B *Boston* MK-III

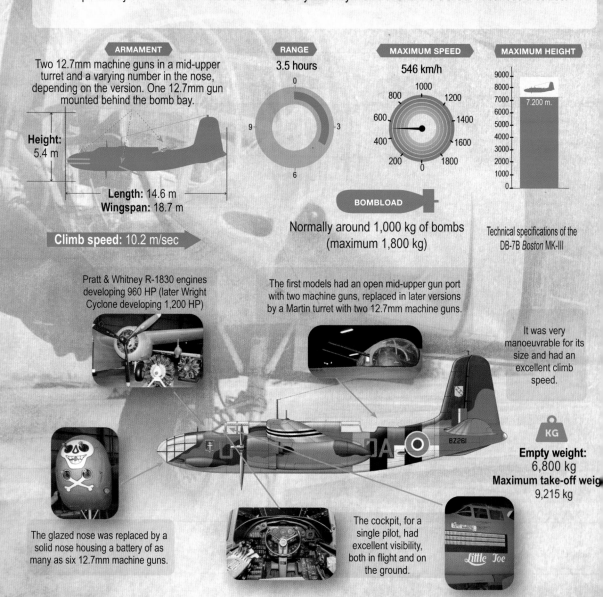

Pratt & Whitney R-1830 engines developing 960 HP (later Wright Cyclone developing 1,200 HP)

The first models had an open mid-upper gun port with two machine guns, replaced in later versions by a Martin turret with two 12.7mm machine guns.

It was very manoeuvrable for its size and had an excellent climb speed.

BZ261

KG

Empty weight:
6,800 kg
Maximum take-off weig
9,215 kg

The glazed nose was replaced by a solid nose housing a battery of as many as six 12.7mm machine guns.

The cockpit, for a single pilot, had excellent visibility, both in flight and on the ground.

Little Joe

MARTIN B-26 *MARAUDER*

Despite its excellent performance, the *Marauder* initially acquired a bad reputation as an accident prone aircraft which was hard to fly, but the problems were soon solved and it became a favourite with aircrews.

Its first mission, on 14 May 1943 with the 322nd Group of the Eighth Air Force, was very promising but three days later ten aircraft were shot down by flak. As well as various groups of the Eighth Air Force, the B-26 equipped many units of the Ninth Air Force, providing tactical support for the invasion.

The B-26 made nearly 130,000 sorties and dropped 170,000 tons of bombs in the European theatre. A total of 911 aircraft were lost in battle or through accidents. In return they shot down 400 enemy aircraft with their defensive armament.

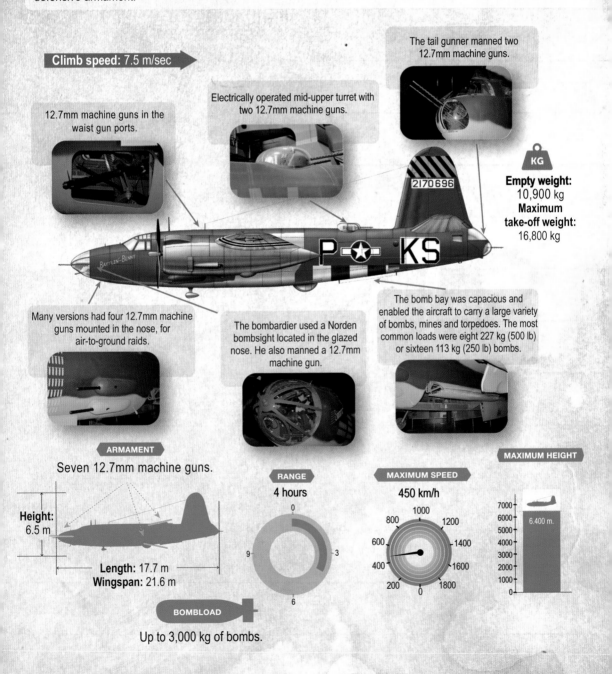

Climb speed: 7.5 m/sec

The tail gunner manned two 12.7mm machine guns.

Electrically operated mid-upper turret with two 12.7mm machine guns.

12.7mm machine guns in the waist gun ports.

KG
Empty weight:
10,900 kg
Maximum take-off weight:
16,800 kg

2170696

P ★ KS

Many versions had four 12.7mm machine guns mounted in the nose, for air-to-ground raids.

The bombardier used a Norden bombsight located in the glazed nose. He also manned a 12.7mm machine gun.

The bomb bay was capacious and enabled the aircraft to carry a large variety of bombs, mines and torpedoes. The most common loads were eight 227 kg (500 lb) or sixteen 113 kg (250 lb) bombs.

ARMAMENT
Seven 12.7mm machine guns.

RANGE
4 hours

MAXIMUM SPEED
450 km/h

MAXIMUM HEIGHT
6.400 m.

Height:
6.5 m

Length: 17.7 m
Wingspan: 21.6 m

BOMBLOAD
Up to 3,000 kg of bombs.

Lack of oxygen was another hazard, even though regulations called for oxygen equipment to be used at over 3,000 metres. There were many accidents due to equipment malfunctions; the Eighth Air Force reported nearly a hundred deaths caused by anoxia, most in the first year of operations. But over half the aircrews would experience more or less critical periods of hypoxia. The tail gunner was the most at risk, being completely isolated from the rest of the crew.

The cancellation of an operation was a serious blow to morale. The worst moments for the aircrews were the periods of waiting before take-off. An aborted

AIRFIELDS

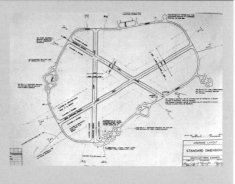

In September 1942 American engineers began constructing seven airfields for the Eighth Air Force. The most common type, known as Class A, consisted of three runways arranged in a triangular pattern, the longest with a minimum length of 1,900 metres and the other two 1,300 metres long. The main runway, used for instrument landing, was oriented according to the prevailing winds. All were 45 metres wide. A 15 metre wide perimeter track ran around the outside of the airfield, with an average length of 4.5 kilometres. Hardstands for the bombers were placed along the outside of the perimeter track.

As well as runways they built hangars (the most common model, the T2, measured 80 × 40 metres), a more or less standard control tower, and quarters for the aircrews. These tended to be "Nissen" huts, although there were other types such as "Laing", "Janes" and "Thorne". These constructions were not particularly comfortable, nor were they suitable for the harsh British winters, but there was no other alternative. Eight men lived in the officers' huts and between twenty-four and thirty-six in the NCOs' huts, which were larger. They consisted of half-cylinders of corrugated steel sitting on metal sheets, heated by coal stoves and poorly ventilated. The smell inside was a mixture of damp, sweat, tobacco and unwashed clothing.

The construction of a typical airfield required uprooting 1,500 trees and nearly 15 kilometres of hedges, excavating 400,000 cubic metres of earth, and building  15 kilometres of roads, not to mention another 15 kilometres of cables, 10 of water pipes, and 6 of drains. Among other materials, the runways required 170,000 cubic metres of concrete and the buildings needed four and a half million bricks.

mission, even after take-off, did not count towards the number of missions needed to complete a tour of duty. Under the original system a crew member had to complete twenty-five missions before being sent home. Later the number would be increased to thirty and then to thirty-five.

1942 ended on an inconclusive note. The Eighth Air Force had initially proved able to bomb with relative precision by day, but at a price that was growing dramatically. Its very existence depended on the top-level strategic decisions that were about to be taken in North Africa. The Germans had started to adapt to the new threat and to develop tactics and aircraft better suited to taking on the *Flying Fortresses*.

Pilot's flying jacket.

The mid-upper turret of a B-17.

The inside of the control tower and a view of the Nissen huts of a typical airfield of the Eighth Air Force.

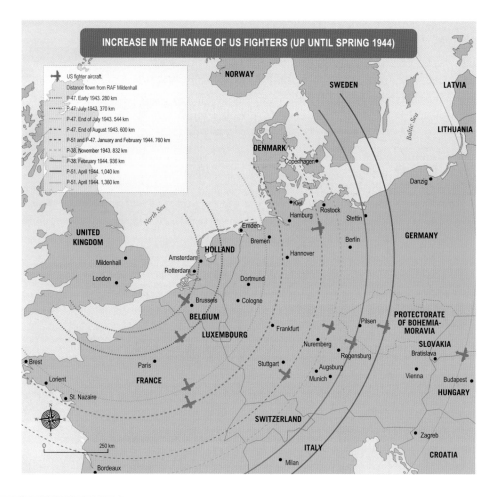

INCREASE IN THE RANGE OF US FIGHTERS (UP UNTIL SPRING 1944)

US fighter aircraft.
Distance flown from RAF Mildenhall
P-47. Early 1943. 280 km
P-47. July 1943. 370 km
P-47. End of July 1943. 544 km
P-47. End of August 1943. 600 km
P-51 and P-47. January and February 1944. 760 km
P-38. November 1943. 832 km
P-38. February 1944. 936 km
P-51. April 1944. 1,040 km
P-51. April 1944. 1,360 km

At the Casablanca Conference in January 1943, Churchill pressured the Americans to join in with the night offensive, preferably under the control of the RAF. Arnold and Eaker were vehemently opposed to the idea, arguing that their units were not prepared for it and that such a course of action would cause the invasion to fail. In a private conversation with Churchill, Eaker was able to convince him of the advantages of maintaining a daylight offensive while the RAF continued with their night raids. As things turned out, the new year would be a most dramatic time for the Eighth Air Force.

A TYPICAL MISSION

The day of a typical mission would start at half past three or four in the morning, when an NCO would wake up the officers and the NCOs in their separate quarters. Breakfast was at half past four and the briefing at a quarter past five. After the briefing the aircrews were taken in trucks to pick up their gear and from there they went to their aircraft. The mechanics (three per aircraft) would be making the final checks and adjustments (they would have been at their posts since three in the morning). Previously the bombs and ammunition would have been loaded.

The aircrew boarded the aircraft either through the aft hatch in the side of the fuselage or through the hatch under the flight deck. It would still be an hour before take-off. The pilot and the chief mechanic made a final visual inspection of the aircraft and its most important systems.

Once these final checks had been made, the pilot opened the side window and started to fire up the engines. The chocks were removed from the wheels and a green light indicated that the aircraft was good to go.

The aircraft taxied in line to the head of the runway from where they took off, laden down with a full fuel and bomb load. Take-off speed was around 170 km/h and the aircraft would take to the air when the end of the runway was already in sight, a moment of great anxiety. This was followed by another dangerous moment when the sky was cloudy, a common situation in England. The cloud cover sometimes reached as high as 6,000 metres forcing the pilots to fly blind, during which time there was a real risk of collision with other aircraft.

Once above the clouds, the aircraft formed up in their pre-established formation and headed for a radio beacon on the coast, where they would join up with the other groups before heading towards their target.

The gunners tested their weapons over the North Sea. All the crew wore harnesses for parachutes which were stored close to their positions. They also wore life vests known as "Mae West" due to their frontal protuberances. The aircraft's cockpit and nose had a rudimentary heating system but the rear section had nothing, so the aircrew protected themselves against the cold the best they could. Some had electrically heated boots, gloves and flying suits but they were in the minority.

The temperature would fall to -40 °C and in those conditions they had to be at their posts and on the alert constantly for the appearance of enemy fighters.

Once close to the target the pilot handed control over to the bombardier who steered the aircraft in the final run-in, choosing the precise moment to drop the bombs. If the main target was covered by clouds, they headed for an alternative one. Anti-aircraft fire was feared the most because there was nothing they could do about it except pray they were not hit. In those final moments, flying in formation, no change of course was possible; it was necessary to fly in a straight line towards the target.

After dropping their bombs the aircraft regrouped and set off for home, which was when they tended to be targeted by enemy fighters. Those that managed to get back, once over England set a course to their home base if they could, where after landing they had a bite to eat before reporting on the details of the mission. If they had wounded men on board they would be attended to immediately and evacuated by ambulance.

9

1943: A Dramatic Year

Despite the new directive the strategic offensive over German territory would not begin until six months later, since the main threat to the Allies were U-boats. Since attacking their Atlantic bases was pointless due to their formidable bunkers and defences, the target would be the shipyards, in combination with Bomber Command's night raids. There were four key targets: Wilhelmshaven, Kiel, Bremen and Vegesack. On 27 January 1943 the first attack was carried out on Wilhelmshaven; the first raid by the Eighth Air Force over German territory.

The B-17s were being joined by the new B-24 *Liberator*. This four-engine bomber actually had a larger payload, better performance figures, and was manufactured in greater numbers than any other bomber of the time, but it would never achieve the reputation of the legendary B-17. Ninety-one B-17s and B-24s took off but only fifty-five found the target, on which they inflicted serious damage. The German fighters were totally surprised by the firepower, the size, and the sturdiness of the bombers and were only able to shoot down three of them while losing seven aircraft of their own.

Flying mitten gloves of a B-17 crew member.

THE POINTBLANK DIRECTIVE

On 21 January 1943 a new directive was released to provide guidance for the Eighth Air Force's bombing operations. It began thus: "*Your primary object will be the progressive destruction and dislocation of the German military, industrial and economic system, and the undermining of the morale of the German people to a point where their capacity for armed resistance is fatally weakened*." Eaker did not actually believe that bombing could break the morale of the people but the objective was included as a necessary sop to the British.

Depending on weather conditions and tactical considerations, the targets were prioritized as follows:

1.- Submarine construction factories.
2.- Aeronautical industry facilities.
3.- Communication nodes.
4.- Oil refineries.
5.- Other military industry targets.
6.- Other targets: submarine bases and the city of Berlin.

The role of the air forces would be to attack Germany by day to destroy targets that were not feasible for night attacks, to keep the pressure up on the morale of the German population, to inflict heavy losses on German day fighters, and to draw German forces away from the Russian and Italian theatres. When the invasion was launched, the Eighth Air Force was to provide every possible support.

Due to bad weather, a month would pass before it was possible to attack the same target again. A number of raids were carried out against the facilities where U-boats were being built but the actual results were very poor. However, the press blew up the results, giving the impression that the bombing raids had destroyed shipyards and submarine bases alike. Arnold and Eaker encouraged this fairy tale, more concerned with strengthening the Eighth Air Force's position than with recognizing the true reality. They were very aware that to a certain extent the only way to achieve a decisive victory from the air was by using a far greater number of

On 28 July the *Luftwaffe* were surprised by the appearance of *Thunderbolts* fitted with their new 100 gallon drop tanks, waiting at the Dutch border for the returning bombers.

aircraft than was available at the time, and that propaganda was a very effective tool for obtaining those much-needed resources.

The day-to-day reality facing the aircrews was very different. The increasingly deeper raids into German territory without a fighter escort caused the number of aircraft losses to creep up and the aircrews' chances of survival to drop alarmingly. By the end of the year the 305th Group had lost half its aircrews and in the other three initial groups only 20 per cent of the original crew members were left. Replacements were scarce and sick and even lightly wounded men were flying combat missions. The morale of the aircrews began to be seriously compromised.

AIRCREW TRAINING

In 1938 the *Army Air Corps* had 21,000 men; by the time of the attack on Pearl Harbor this figure had risen to 350,000, and 18 months later the figure was 2.1 million. How were these men trained?

In January 1942 the minimum age for an officer was lowered from 20 to 18 years old. Candidates had to pass a written exam and be in good physical shape. Up until December 1942 all were volunteers. After that date there was a certain amount of conscription but the percentage of volunteers remained very high so the recruiters could choose the best candidates. The pay was good, around 1,800 dollars a year, with a 50 per cent flying bonus for a second-lieutenant (a four-star general's salary was around 8,000 dollars). The average young American was excited by aviation at that time, and there was no lack of candidates.

After a full psychological and physical exam, candidates were classified for training as pilots, navigators or bomb-aimbers. Around 50 per cent of the candidates failed to make the grade and were sent either to the Army or to aerial gunner school to fly as NCOs.

Those that passed were sent on a two month basic training course after which they went to a flying school. There were three levels (elementary, basic and advanced), each lasting around 9-10 weeks. Finally they attended a final course specific to the aircraft they would be flying, also lasting around ten weeks. The learning process was not without risk. At the training centres some 15,000 airmen and candidates died in accidents during the war. Only 60 per cent of the flying school trainees finished the courses.

CONSOLIDATED B-24 *LIBERATOR*

More of these bombers were built than any other. Although technologically more advanced than the B-17, it was eclipsed by the latter's glamour. It was exhausting to fly but could carry a heavier bombload further, although it was not as sturdy as the B-17.

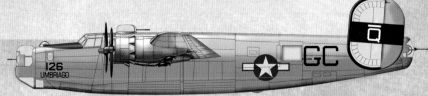

Electrically powered rear turret, with two 12.7mm machine guns.

12.7mm machine guns in the waist gun ports.

Twin turret with two 12.7mm guns located aft of the cockpit

The initial versions did not have a nose turret; from version J on they all had one.

At either end of the tailplane there were large rounded tail fins, on which twin rudders were mounted.

The bombardier's position was in the nose. In early versions he also manned a machine gun in the glazed nose cone.

It could carry up to 2,000 pounds of bombs in the bomb bay, which had two racks separated by a catwalk.

On the flight deck sat the pilot/commander and the co-pilot while the navigator travelled further forward, between the flight deck and the front turret/nose cone.

Twin-row 14 cylinder Pratt & Whitney engines delivering 1,200 HP, fitted with a General Electric B-2 turbocharger for high altitude flying.

18,325 aircraft of this type were built, and they operated in every theatre (12,731 B-17s were built). The design of the wing was its most characteristic feature; its high aspect ratio wing gave it plenty of lift. It carried out 226,775 missions in Europe, dropping 462,508 tons of bombs. A third of these aircraft were destroyed.

Climb speed: 5.2 m/sec 6000 m in 22 minutes

ARMAMENT

Ten 12.7mm machine guns
The ball turret is retractable and so does not appear in the profile view.

Height: 5.5 m

Length: 20.5 m
Wingspan: 33.3 m
Wing area: 98 m²

RANGE
7 hours

MAXIMUM SPEED
470 km/h

MAXIMUM HEIGHT
9.000 m.

BOMBLOAD

Up to 6,000 kg of bombs, although the normal load was 3-4 tons. With 1,200 kg the range was 2,000 km. The normal bombload was no more than 4,000 kg.

KG

Empty weight:
15,430 kg
Maximum take-off weight:
29,500 kg

Propulsion:
Four Pratt & Whitney
R-1830-65 engines producing 1,200 HP

Aircrew:
10 men

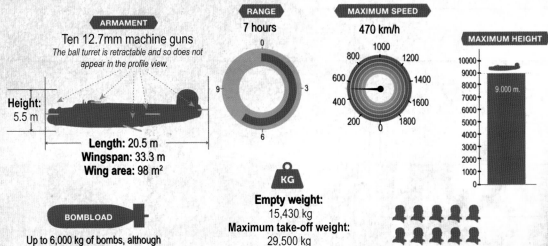

M-2

The main defensive weapon of American bombers was the M-2 12.7mm machine gun. With a firing rate of around 550 rpm (rounds per minute) it had a maximum effective range of about 800 metres, better than the range of the machine guns carried by enemy fighters.

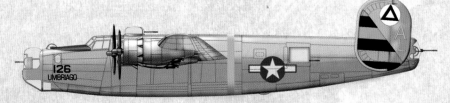

Many airmen suffered from symptoms of stress and anxiety, what would later come to be known as battle fatigue or combat stress: nightmares, insomnia, mood swings, irritability, tremors, impotence, aggressive behaviour, and high alcohol consumption, among others. Some weekend dances turned into veritable pitched battles sparked by trivial incidents. A psychiatric study showed that all airmen who had completed their 25 mission tour of duty exhibited at least one serious symptom of battle fatigue.

Many cases were actually due to simple fatigue and could be "cured" with rest and some days off. These cases were diagnosed as "flying fatigue". What was then known as "operational fatigue" affected men who had gone through very traumatic experiences and had been exposed to excessive stress over a long time. These cases required psychiatric treatment and recovery was slower. The third category of psychological disorder occurred very infrequently. This was when a crew member broke down after his first missions. Commanders treated such men as cowards. If they were officers they were given the option of resigning and if they were NCOs they were stripped of their rank and assigned to ground duties.

1. Accidents when damaged aircraft tried to land were very frequent.

2. Loading up with bombs before a mission.

3. The B-17 could withstand considerable damage.

4. P-38 Lightning escort fighter.

In the first year of operations, the Eighth Air Force suffered around 1,300 wounded in action and over 1,600 cases of frostbite.

Military psychiatrists came to the conclusion that there was no such thing as "adaptation to combat". Nobody ever got used to it. Sooner or later any man will break down as a result of repeated exposure to combat stress. Arnold, who had nearly died in a flying accident when he was one of the pioneers of aviation, understood this situation very well, because it had taken him four years to fly again. Courage is a limited asset. Every man, however brave and well-trained he is, has limited reserves of courage which can run out if he is repeatedly exposed to situations of extreme stress and danger.

The life of an airman was one of enormous contrasts, in which long periods of almost civilian life alternated with moments of huge stress and danger, during which on many occasions he had no way of fighting back. When faced with flak all he could do was hunker down at his post and hope that the shrapnel would respect him and that the aircraft would not take a direct hit.

As far as possible less serious cases were treated on the base, where simply sharing living quarters with a group of fellow airmen could be a great help. Later, when the number of missions per tour

AN EXAMPLE OF GROUP MORALE

Four NCOs of a bomber swore an oath that they would never leave any member of the group behind. On a mission some weeks later the aircraft was hit by flak and the pilot gave the order to bail out. The belly gunner was trapped in his turret a the other three who had sworn the oath told him they would die with him. And they did. All the crew members bailed out except for the four friends who remained together until the aircraft crashed into the ground.

MEMPHIS BELLE

The B-17 *Memphis Belle* of the 91st Group flew its first mission on 7 November 1942, commanded by Captain Robert Morgan from North Carolina. His first target was the submarine base at Brest.

The aircraft was named after Morgan's sweetheart at the time, Margaret Polk, whom he had met during training at Walla Walla, Washington. The pinup drawing and the name caught the eye of film director William Wyler, who was very impressed by the striking decorations that the airmen painted on their aircraft. It was something not previously seen, not just in other countries but not even in the US Navy and Army. They were veritable symbols of life and individuality in a brutal and depersonalized war. Wyler flew in the *Memphis Belle* to shoot some memorable footage which would be used in a propaganda film that became very famous at the time.

The *Memphis Belle* would popularly become the first bomber whose aircrew completed twenty-five missions and could return home. In fact the first aircraft to achieve this was *Hell's Angels* on 14 May. The *Belle* would follow three days later and Billy Wilder, who had very good contacts, arranged things so it would be the *Belle* that featured in his documentary which would receive all the fame. Its last mission was over Lorient.

After their return, Morgan and nine members of the Eighth Air Force, not of the original aircrew, made a tour of 31 cities of the United States. Morgan married, not his former sweetheart Margaret but one Dotty Johnson whom he met on the tour. Later he trained with the new B-29 bombers and was posted to the Marianas from where he took part in the bombing offensive against Japan. He christened his aircraft *Dauntless Dotty*.

Billy Wilder would direct the famous movie *Memphis Belle*, which would become a great commercial success, despite certain inaccuracies and licenses taken. He would later direct the film *Thunderbolt* for the Air Force, and, in 1946 he directed the movie *The Best Years of Our Lives*, about three airmen attempting to return to civilian life.

"If it hadn't been for London, we would have all gone crazy" (Robert Morgan, captain of the *Memphis Belle*).

of duty increased to thirty and, more so in the summer of 1944 when the figure rose to thirty-five, morale began to suffer again. Strong ties were forged among the members of bomber crews which helped strengthen the morale of the entire group. If the skipper also knew how to bring them all together and lead by example the effect was remarkable. Such ties could also exist among aircrews of the same squadron or group, but did not extend to larger units.

Dropping bombs by radar, through the clouds.

When they were on the ground, the aircrew had plenty of opportunities to mix with the civilian population, both in the vicinity of their bases and in London. Leave spent in London was a dream for many of the young men of the Eighth Air Force. The British capital may have been bombed and was gripped by rationing and high inflation, but it was still hugely attractive for young Americans. They were well paid, wore splendid uniforms, had a sense of humour, and were fans of music by Glenn Miller. They were also a source of cigarettes, chocolate and nylon stockings, and they were good dancers of foxtrot and swing, all of which made them highly appealing to young British women. And London for those young airmen was not a place for cultural tourism; it was a place to drink and forget, preferably with female company.

Officers stayed at the best hotels, the Savoy being one of the favourites. They were seldom short of female company. For many London women the young American officers were too big a temptation; they were so different from the average Englishmen of the early 1940s with their staid, quasi-Victorian manners.

Maintaining morale was essential because the Germans were tightening up their defences. Finally, aware of the threat posed by bombers, Göring started to transfer units from the Eastern Front, with the result that from the 260 fighters that the

Luftwaffe deployed on the Western Front in the autumn of 1942, the figure almost doubled by the spring of 1943. The *Flying Fortresses* were still enemies that were hard to knock down. On 18 March 103 aircraft attacked Vegesack and only two were lost, despite the formation being attacked by fifty fighters. The German fighters were finding the concentrated defensive fire from the bombers to be highly dangerous.

The fighters had to take advantage of their enemy's few weak points, which they had been able to identify late in 1942. When the Eighth Air Force attacked Bremen on 17 April it suffered serious losses (fifteen bombers shot down, twice that of previous missions) in what was then their biggest air battle ever. The Germans attacked from the front, taking advantage of the bombers' scant forward-facing firepower, and only lost five aircraft.

The commander of the Eighth Air Force's fighters, *General* Hunter, put up his few *Thunderbolt* fighters in daring raids across the Channel to lure the German fighters into fighting them with the hope of shooting down a significant number of them. Göring's order was categorical; the German fighters were to concentrate on attacking the bombers. The only way to draw the *Luftwaffe* into a battle of attrition would be by using the escort fighters flying with the bombers.

Eaker constantly asked for larger forces, since the number of aircraft he could use on each mission was really low, never over 130 aircraft, not nearly enough to achieve decisive results. He needed many more aircraft in order to maintain regular

PRECISION BOMBING

A box was made up of eighteen aircraft which dropped their bombs when they saw their leader drop theirs. The bombs, dropped from an altitude of 6,500 metres, fell in an area of approximately 500 metres square per box. With clear skies the average circular error probable for the leader's bombs was around 400 metres. With poor visibility this figure grew to nearly 1,200 metres. In the best case scenario only half the bombs would fall within a radius of 400 metres from the target. With poor weather the radius grew to nearly 5 kilometres.

operations over German territory. Most missions attacked targets in France, leaving the German targets for the British. But, despite Arnold's best intentions, North Africa continued to be the priority for the American strategists in terms of the allocation of resources.

Liberators taxiing to the head of the runway.

The first and much needed replacements began to arrive in spring, and started to take part in combat missions in May. The available aircrews doubled in number, from about 100 to 215 by mid-May. During the first ten months of battle the Eighth Air Force had lost 188 aircraft and 1,900 aircrew, without counting those who died after arriving back at base. Three quarters of the original aircrews from autumn 1942 failed to complete their twenty-five tours. On 29 May the largest number of aircraft to date took to the air, a total of 279 four-engine bombers. This signalled the end of what Eaker called the trial period. From that moment on, a continuous offensive could begin against strategic targets in German territory, still without a fighter escort. This belief in the self-sufficiency of the *Flying Fortresses* was not so much due to the pre-war doctrine but rather because of the lack of escort fighters with a long enough range. Such fighters would still be a long time coming, but the need for them began to be obvious to everyone.

The agile *Spitfire* lacked the necessary range and the *Lightning* was not up to the task of taking on German fighters and besides, most were sent to the Mediterranean. The recently arrived P-47 *Thunderbolt* was much better. It was fast, well-armed and sturdy, being able to withstand an incredible amount of damage and continue flying. At first their range only enabled them to escort the bombers to the German border, after which the bombers were on their own. However, until October there would not be enough of these aircraft in operation.

The bombing raids were become increasingly costly in terms of losses of aircraft and men, despite achieving unquestionable successes on many occasions. On 13 June 227 aircraft attacked Bremen and Kiel, of which 26 failed to return. On the 22nd, of the 235 aircraft which attacked industrial targets on the Ruhr, 16 were shot down.

On 1 July *General* Anderson, 37, took command of the Eighth Air Force

"We can wreck Berlin from end to end if the USAAF come in with us. It will cost us between 400 and 500 aircraft. It will cost Germany the war" (Arthur Harris).

bombers while the fighters were entrusted to *Major General* Kepner, an old friend of Eaker's. Both were aggressive leaders, who were expected to pass on their fighting spirit to their airmen. For the last two months the weather had been so bad that operations had been reduced to a minimum, but during the last week of July it all changed.

P-47 *THUNDERBOLT*

The huge *Thunderbolt* was an aircraft literally designed around the engine chosen to power it, which was the 18-cylinder radial Pratt & Whitney R 2800 developing 2,535 HP. The engine's turbocharger was located in the lower fuselage and its size and complicated ductwork made the aircraft very bulky. After some initial difficulties, production started in March 1942. They flew their first escort mission with the Eighth Air Force on 13 April 1943. However, their range at the time was still not enough to enable them to escort bombers over mainland Germany.

Successive versions improved the aircraft's performance and the rate of production increased. Over 12,600 units of the D version alone were built, making it the most numerous American fighter ever. By using three drop tanks the P-47D could escort bombers to numerous targets in the interior of Germany.

The statistics of this aircraft are impressive: their loss rate per mission was 0.7 per cent and they shot down 4.6 enemy aircraft for every plane lost. P-47s of the Eighth Air Force shot down 3,752 German aircraft and destroyed around 3,300 on the ground.

The D type had a maximum speed of nearly 700 km/h and a service ceiling of 12,400 metres. Its range with drop tanks was 3,000 kilometres. Its empty weight was 4.5 tons but fully loaded it weighed close to 8 tons. It was armed with eight 12.7mm Browning machine guns in the wings. It could carry up to 1,150 kilograms of bombs and napalm tanks, and eight rockets.

"We started out with an inferiority complex. Those damned members of Eagle Squadron demoralized us with their pessimism regarding the P-47, when they spoke about those heavy Thunderbolts and the Luftwaffe with their four years of experience... Being able to fight them with their two-ton Spitfires had taken them blood, sweat and tears. They told us: 'You'll die in five missions with those seven-ton birds of yours', and we believed them.

During the first missions we were more concerned with handling the new aircraft than anything else, but soon we came to realize one of the P-47's great advantages, its power. If you got into trouble you opened up the throttles, dived, and that enormous engine got you out of it. We soon gained confidence, especially in dogfights at high altitude."

(Testimony of a *Thunderbolt* pilot)

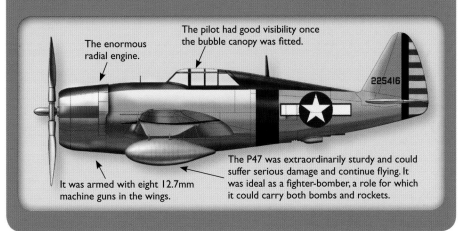

The pilot had good visibility once the bubble canopy was fitted.

The enormous radial engine.

225416

It was armed with eight 12.7mm machine guns in the wings.

The P47 was extraordinarily sturdy and could suffer serious damage and continue flying. It was ideal as a fighter-bomber, a role for which it could carry both bombs and rockets.

JIMMY DOOLITTLE

James Harold "Jimmy" Doolittle was born in California in 1896 but was raised in Alaska. He was one of the pioneers of American aviation and made a number of flights which would make him famous. He was also one of the first men to receive a doctorate in aeronautics from MIT. In 1940 he became president of the Institute of Aeronautical Science.

In 1942, having been recalled from the Reserve, he was promoted to lieutenant colonel and became a media hero when he planned and led the famous Tokyo raid. He took off from the aircraft carrier *Hornet* leading a force of sixteen B-25s, for which he was awarded the Congressional Medal of Honor.

Promoted to the rank of brigadier general, he commanded first the Fifteenth Air Force and, from January 1944, the Eighth Air Force, ending the war in the Pacific theatre. On retirement he returned to his pre-war employer, Shell Oil, as a vice-president and worked as an advisor to the US air forces. He died in 1993.

24 July saw the beginning of what would come to be known as "Blitz Week". The British carried out a savage offensive against Hamburg, during which the first ever firestorm in history was created. Over 50,000 people were burned to death or suffocated. But the Eighth Air Force also contributed to the massacre. On the first day of the week they flew a mission against targets in Norway and then headed to Hamburg. On the 25th and 26th they carried out massed attacks against the city's industrial centres and shipyards. On the night of the 27th the RAF used the Window system for the first time in order to confuse German radar, which proved to be a great success. Around 700 bombers dropped an apocalyptical number of incendiary bombs and two-ton blockbuster bombs on the city centre, destroying entire city blocks and preventing the fire services from reaching the fires. This process would continue until 2 August.

Speer, the architect of the diversification of German industrial production, before the bombing offensive.

Despite all the destruction suffered, over 80 per cent of the production of the factories in the areas bombed were back working within four months, but both Göring and Speer, the German Minister of Armaments, were aware of the enormous power

NORDEN BOMBSIGHT

In 1931, Danish scientist Karl Norden, who had emigrated to the USA in 1904, developed a bombsight designed for bombers attacking naval targets. It enabled the operator to enter the speed of the aircraft and its altitude, so that the device, stabilized by gyroscopes, could calculate the trajectory of the bombs and the moment when they should be dropped. Without the Army's initial knowledge the Navy ordered 90,000 units at a cost of around 10,000 dollars each.

In ideal conditions the bombsight was capable of hitting targets from a height of 7,000 metres within a 30 metre radius. Once close to the target the pilot handed over control of the aircraft to the bombardier, who guided it towards the target using the bombsight. In 1944 the normal procedure was for only the lead aircraft to use the bombsight; the rest of the formation would drop their bombs when the leader did.

of destruction of the Allied heavy bombers. However, in order to destroy large industrial complexes definitively it was clear that it was necessary to use more bombers, for more time, and drop heavier bombs.

The "Blitz Week" had cost the Eighth Air Force dearly: they had lost ninety-seven aircraft, a 10 per cent loss rate. The aircrews were exhausted and needed a rest, especially to prepare for a mission that Eaker had been six months designing.

According to the American pre-war doctrine identifying "legitimate" targets, one of the weak spots of the aeronautical industry were its bearings factories. Nearly 60 per cent of the bearings used in Germany were produced in three factories in Schweinfurt, a small city to the north of Nuremberg. The mission consisted of an attack on the bearings factories, together with a separate attack on a Messerschmitt fighter assembly plant in Regensburg, Bavaria, where one out of three of the fighters were produced. Never had a target so deep into German territory been attacked. But the real novelty of the plan was that, after bombing Regensburg, that part of the force would continue flying southwards to land at airfields in North Africa, thereby avoiding attacks by German fighters on the way home. The Schweinfurt bombers would return to their bases in England. The intention was to confuse German

defences so the bombers could avoid confronting German fighters.

Three groups of *Liberators* were unavailable for this raid. They had been sent to Libya to prepare for another mission, initially scheduled for 1 August, that would become legendary; the attack on the refineries at Ploesti, Romania, where 60 per cent of the oil consumed by Germany was produced.

These three strategic targets had been chosen by a group of experts at the Pentagon, based on economic theories and following a pre-war doctrine. According to this doctrine there were industrial bottlenecks whose neutralization could paralyze the entire war industry (for example, bearings factories). If attacks were concentrated on those critical points, the results would be far more effective than those achieved by bombing dispersed targets.

1. P-47Ds in formation.

2. Fighter pilots sitting on the wing of a *Thunderbolt*.

3. Formation of B-24s on their way to the target, flying very low over the sea.

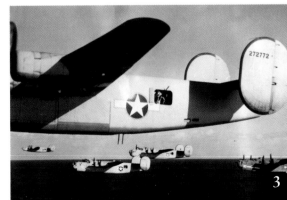

In August Anderson finally launched the Eighth Air Force's hitherto most ambitious operation; the dual attack on Regensburg and Schweinfurt which, while it was presented as a great victory (and it certainly caused enough damage to anger Hitler and worry Speer), it was actually a catastrophe for the Eighth Air Force. Forty per cent of the attacking force was lost. Another operation like that and the unit would cease to exist.

REGENSBURG AND SCHWEINFURT

On 17 August 1943 the aircrews rose at half past one in the morning. Breakfast was especially generous. During the briefing session, the targets were explained to the astonishment of the aircrews. Never had they flown so deeply into the heart of Germany. And for those that would be continuing on to Africa, the experience was even more of a surprise. In order to increase their range the B-17s had been fitted with drop tanks, known as "Tokyo tanks".

The force that would attack Regensburg (led by LeMay) consisted of 146 B-17s and would have a fighter escort as far as the fighters' range would allow. The 230 aircraft which would attack Schweinfurt (led by Williams) would take off a little later and the two forces would fly together before separating over Germany with the idea of confusing the German fighters. The Regensburg force would attract most of the fighters but then would flee south over the Alps. The Schweinfurt force would be able to reach the target undisturbed but would have fighters to contend with on the way home.

At half past five the bombers were waiting at the head of the runway for the dense fog covering the airfields to lift. The weather over the target was excellent but they could not take off in those conditions. Since the fog failed to lift, Anderson decided to change the timing in order to avoid collisions while they climbed. The Regensburg force took off first followed by the Schweinfurt group much later, taking most of the *Thunderbolt* escort with them.

When over Belgium, still 450 kilometres away from their target, the escort fighters turned around and German fighters homed in on the B-17s. In a few minutes six Fortresses were shot down. Another eight met the same fate in the following half hour.

An hour later they reached their target and dropped their bombs from 6,000 metres, nearly without opposition. Each bomber dropped ten 250 kg bombs, many of which hit the target, killing some 400 workers.

They then headed at full speed towards the Alps, around 100 kilometres away. From there, now safe from German fighters, they still had another five hours' flying to North Africa. 240 airmen did not make it. Two bombers, with serious damage, landed in Switzerland, where the crew were interned. Those that reached Libya would fly back to England some weeks later, bombing targets around Bordeaux on the way. But another 55 B-17s with irreparable damage would remain in Libya for ever.

The force targeting Schweinfurt took off when the fog lifted and, once over Belgium and without a fighter escort, they were met by around 300 German fighters, over twice the number that had attacked LeMay's force. The Germans were operating very close to their bases, so they could land, take on fresh ammunition, and attack the bombers again. Some fighters flew three sorties that day.

Unlike at Regensburg, the bombing was very inaccurate. Also, the 250 kg and 500 kg bombs were not big enough to destroy the machine tools. Often the bombs only destroyed the buildings, but their contents survived in a condition to start working again within a very short time. In total 265 tons of high explosive bombs were dropped and 115 tons of incendiaries. Initially, bearing production dropped by 38 per cent but very soon recovered. Thirty-six Fortresses failed to return (21 were shot down on the outward run, two over the target, and thirteen more on the return trip). The survivors began landing in England at six in the evening.

The press blew up the results, reporting that only two bombers had been lost in return for 288 German aircraft shot down. The reality was very different. Sixty B-17s were shot down and another hundred or so were so badly damaged that they never flew again. This represented 40 per cent of the original force. Actual losses of the Luftwaffe totalled forty-seven aircraft. But Hitler was furious and blamed Jeschonnek, Chief of Staff of the Luftwaffe. Jeschonnek would later commit suicide on 19 August.

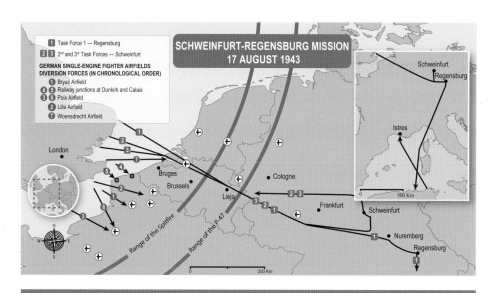

COMPOSITION OF THE ATTACK FORCE

Schweinfurt: 1st Bombardment Wing (Brigadier Robert B. Williams)

3rd Task Force (Colonel Turner)	
103rd Combat Wing:	103rd Group (17 aircraft)
	379th Group (18 aircraft)
	303rd Group (18 aircraft)
102nd Combat Wing:	305th Group (20 aircraft)
	306th Group (21 aircraft)
	92nd Group (20 aircraft)
2nd Task Force (Colonel Gross)	
Combined Wing:	306th Group (20 aircraft)
	351st Group (21 aircraft)
	384th Group (19 aircraft)
101st Combat Wing:	101st Group (19 aircraft)
	91st Group (18 aircraft)
	381st Group (20 aircraft)

Between each Task Force there would be a theoretical twenty minute gap and between each Combat Wing a five minute gap.

Regensburg: 4th Bombardment Wing (Col. Curtis E. LeMay)

402nd Combat Wing:	95th Group (21 aircraft)
	100th Group (21 aircraft)
401st Combat Wing:	94th Group (21 aircraft)
	385th Group (21 aircraft)
403rd Combat Wing:	390th Group (21 aircraft)
	96th Group (21 aircraft)
	388th Group (21 aircraft)

The gap between each wing was three minutes.

Hitler now started to take the air defence of the *Reich* more seriously. Fighter production doubled in 1943 and was even higher the following year. However, losses were very heavy. In August 1943 alone 334 fighters were lost over the Western Front and, to make matters worse, experienced pilots were being lost. In fact, taking into account the casualties among veteran pilots, Regensburg-Schweinfurt was starting to look like a defeat for both sides.

Bombs away!

For two weeks the Eighth Air Force did not venture beyond the range of the fighter escorts. On 6 September Stuttgart was attacked; the city was covered by a thick layer of clouds and most of the aircraft dropped their bombs on the way home. This fiasco cost the Eighth Air Force forty-five bombers; many were shot down but others crashed into the English Channel when they ran out of fuel.

Although one squadron of bombers joined the RAF in eight night missions, the Eighth Air Force remained faithful to its principles, awaiting the arrival of long-range escort fighters. In September the Eighth was reorganized; the 1st, 2nd and 4th Bomb Wings became the 1st, 2nd, and 3rd Bomb Divisions respectively. The 2nd Bomb Division only flew *Liberators*.

The better weather in October prompted Eaker to launch another offensive which would come to be known as "Black Week". On 8 October he attacked facilities in the Bremen-Vegesack sector and on the following day aircraft factories to the north of Berlin and at Marienburg. On the 10th it was Münster's turn. Eighty-eight bombers were lost in those operations and many more sustained heavy damaged. The 100th Group lost twelve out of thirteen aircraft and over half their aircrews.

On the 14th Schweinfurt was attacked once again with over 300 aircraft which were met by opposition of a kind never before encountered. Not only single-engine fighters, but also twin-engine Me 110s and Ju 88s armed with rockets attacked the *Flying Fortresses*, shooting sixty of them down while another seventeen crashed on landing. It was the biggest air battle of the war so far and only thirty-three bombers landed unscathed.

Late in October the situation hung in the balance. Neither side had air superiority. The Eighth Air Force was suffering very heavy losses (an average of twenty-eight bombers per mission) but none of the attacks had been turned back and the Germans had lost nearly 250 fighters in the month of October alone, 17 per cent of its forces in the West.

The *Thunderbolts* began to operate with new drop tanks that increased their range to reach a good number of Germany's more western cities. But Göring was loath to admit such a thing. In a tense argument with Galland, the latter told Göring that several American fighters had been shot down over Aachen and that the wreckage was there to prove it. Without any evidence of his own to refute such a claim, Göring went as far as to give Galland an official order instructing him that US fighters *"had not reached Aachen..."*

1 and 2. Some of the B-17's defensive armament.

3. Aircraft flying towards their target.

4. The nose of the B-17 proved to be very vulnerable, so later a twin-gun chin turret was installed below the nose.

5. The B-24H was fitted with a nose turret with two 12.7mm machine guns.

GERMAN DAYLIGHT FIGHTERS

The bombers had two major enemies when flying over Europe: anti-aircraft defences and German fighters. There were basically two types of German day fighters: the Me 109 and the Fw 190, both manufactured in various versions

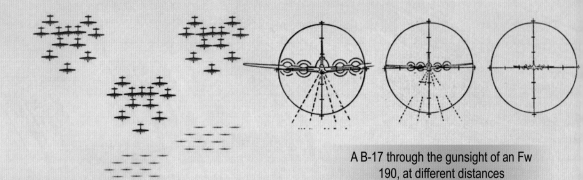

A B-17 through the gunsight of an Fw 190, at different distances

In addition to these two single-engine day fighters there were night fighters, which were vastly inferior when it came to engaging escort fighters. The most effective night fighters were the Me 110 and the Ju 88, both heavily

armed with cannons and some carrying rockets of up to 210mm calibre with the aim of splitting up the close bomber formations.

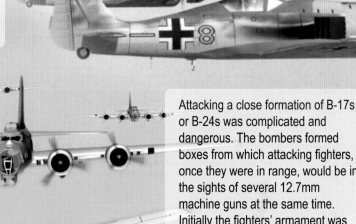

Attacking a close formation of B-17s or B-24s was complicated and dangerous. The bombers formed boxes from which attacking fighters, once they were in range, would be in the sights of several 12.7mm machine guns at the same time. Initially the fighters' armament was upgraded (more 20mm cannons or 13mm machine guns) but that had a negative effect on the aircraft's performance.

Me 109G

The Me 109G could be fitted with a 20mm cannon in the prop shaft and two under the wings, as well as two 13mm machine guns on the cowling. It was fast and in good hands would be a formidable opponent until the end of the war, although it required the pilot to be alert at all times and by 1943 it was already an obsolescent design (it had flown for the first time in 1935). Over 35,000 planes were built.

Climb speed: 20 m/sec

The cockpit was a little narrow and visibility on landing was not good.

The 1,475 HP engine's injection system gave it an advantage over its rivals in some manoeuvres.

The undercarriage, with its wheels too close together, was one of its weak points.

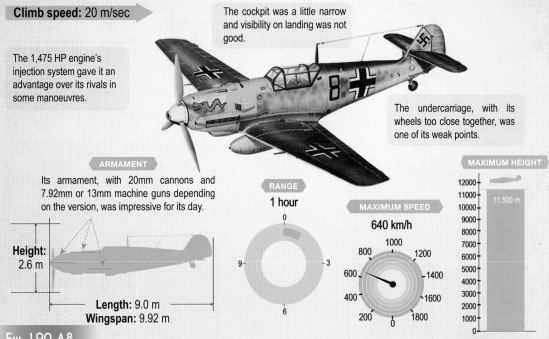

ARMAMENT

Its armament, with 20mm cannons and 7.92mm or 13mm machine guns depending on the version, was impressive for its day.

RANGE

1 hour

MAXIMUM SPEED

640 km/h

MAXIMUM HEIGHT

11.500 m.

Height: 2.6 m

Length: 9.0 m
Wingspan: 9.92 m

Fw 190 A8

The Fw 190 A-4 was armed with four 20mm cannons and two 7.92mm machine guns. An average of 20 hits were needed to shoot down a *Flying Fortress*. An average pilot only managed a 2 per cent hit rate, so it would need 1,000 rounds to achieve 20 hits, but an Fw 190 only carried 510 rounds. The cannons were not effective over a range of more than 500 metres but fire from the B-17's 12.7mm machine guns was effective against fighters for up to nearly 1,000 metres. Over 20,000 units of all versions of the Fw 190 would be built, the most advanced being the Ta 152.

ARMAMENT

The Fw 190 was very well-armed, with four 20mm cannons and two machine guns.

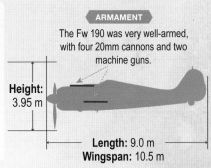

Height: 3.95 m

Length: 9.0 m
Wingspan: 10.5 m

The canopy afforded the pilot excellent visibility in dogfights.

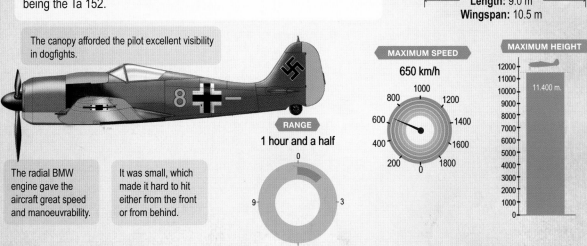

MAXIMUM SPEED

650 km/h

RANGE

1 hour and a half

MAXIMUM HEIGHT

11.400 m.

The radial BMW engine gave the aircraft great speed and manoeuvrability.

It was small, which made it hard to hit either from the front or from behind.

Germany had no oil resources and had developed a vast synthetic oil production system in the interior of the *Reich*, which was well dispersed and protected. The main sources of oil were the Romanian oil fields, and the Ploesti refinery complex about 50 kilometres from Bucharest was essential for refining the oil they produced.

A gross intelligence blunder led the Americans to believe that Ploesti was lightly defended when in fact it was one of the most heavily defended sites in Europe. The man responsible for planning the mission was Colonel Jacob Smart, an advisor to Arnold. He proposed surprising the Germans with a low-level attack. Instead of a high-altitude precision bombing raid, the *Liberators*, taking off from bases in Libya, would fly at low level to their target. Dropping bombs at an altitude of between 70 and 200 metres, flying at 300 km/h, accuracy would be very high and the aircraft would be a hard target for the anti-aircraft defences since they would be in range of each gun for a very short time. Also the aircrews would have a better chance of surviving if they had to make a forced landing.

Only the *Liberator* had range enough for the mission. But it was less sturdy than the B-17 and harder to manoeuvre at low altitude, which made the mission all the more risky. Five groups of bombers would attack, two from the Ninth Air Force and three from the Eighth, the 44th and the 93rd, both veteran units, and the 389th which had recently arrived from the United States.

After twelve days of low-level flight training, on Sunday, 1 August 178 *Liberators* took off and headed towards their target. They called themselves the "Zero Raiders".

A number of navigation errors and the presence of high cumulus nimbus clouds caused coordination to break down and the various groups arrived at the target individually.

Ploesti was extraordinarily well defended. Over fifty 88mm batteries and 100 light 20mm and 37mm guns protected the complex, together with around 250 single- and twin-engine fighters stationed nearby. Two thousand smoke generators completed the defences.

Navigation errors caused two groups to attack secondary targets and only three groups found the primary target, but they arrived in dribs and drabs so that the defenders could pick them off one by one. Instead of a massed surprise attack that would overwhelm the defences, the *Liberators* arrived in small groups, flying through dense clouds of smoke caused by the fires that the first aircraft had started.

In twenty-seven minutes it was all over. The surviving *Liberators* were spread out over a hundred kilometres along the Danube Valley and were attacked by a large number of fighters. Over half of the bombers ran out of ammunition and others were severely damaged. Around thirteen hours after take-off the first bombers started to land at the Libyan airfields.

The attack destroyed half of the refineries' production capacity but they were only working at half capacity so that in a few weeks production was back up to higher than it had been before the raid. Only a hundred or so civilians died.

But forty-six aircraft were shot down and fifty-three seriously damaged. Only thirty-three returned in a condition to take to the air again soon. In total, 310 airmen were killed, 130 wounded, and over 100 captured. Five Congressional Medals of Honor were awarded.

In this battle of attrition both sides were losing and nothing was decided. But the Allies had a very clear objective; Eisenhower needed air superiority to guarantee the success of the invasion, Operation Overlord. And to achieve this it seemed that the best way was to sacrifice heavy bombers in order to lure the German fighters into the air. Both sides would suffer high losses, but the Americans could replace theirs while the Germans could not, especially not their well-trained and experienced pilots. For the American strategists it was preferable to lose several hundred bombers in the air rather than several divisions on the beaches of Normandy.

During the months of November and December the weather worsened to such an extent that precision bombing missions were rendered virtually impossible. If they had been possible, they would still have been flying without an adequate fighter escort since Eaker continued to be convinced of the self-sufficiency of his heavy bombers and Arnold was eager to convert the Air Force into a fully

A B-24 destroyed by flak.

independent unit. And that depended on the Eighth Air Force demonstrating clearly that daylight strategic bombing was possible and effective.

But the weather was not on their side. In November the Eighth Air Force tried bombing by radar and the result was very poor. On the 3rd a force of 566 bombers and 378 fighters (*Lightning* and *Thunderbolt* with the new drop tanks) attacked Wilhelmshaven from an overcast sky. The mere appearance of such a force was a matter of grave consternation for Galland. The Americans had replaced their losses with amazing speed and were flying blind, in conditions that until then had rendered operations impossible.

The lead aircraft were equipped with H2X radars, a version of the British H2S, for locating targets. Bombing was not very accurate but it was a good example of the potential of new technologies which gave the Allies an even greater advantage.

BLACK WEEK

On 14 October, 300 bombers attacked Schweinfurt and were met by around 300 German aircraft. Among them were twin-engine Me 110s and Ju 88s armed with 210mm rockets which were fired from over a kilometre away and exploded in the middle of the formation of bombers. A direct hit could destroy a B-17 but it was a very rare occurrence. What the rockets did achieve was to cause the bombers to take evasive action and so disrupt the compact formations. This resulted

in some aircraft becoming isolated from the formation when they became easy pickings for the German fighters, which would converge on them from all sides to finish them off.

By the end of the day, seventy-seven Fortresses had been destroyed (some due to direct hits by rockets) but the Germans lost nearly 100 aircraft. Bomber aircrew losses were horrendous: 642 of a total of 2,900 airmen, an intolerable 22 per cent.

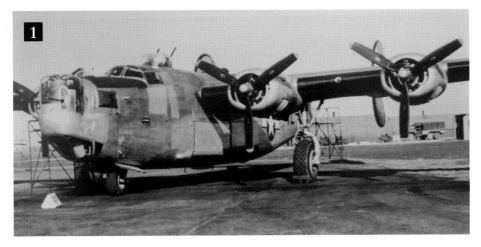

1. A B-24 which returned unscathed.

2. Briefing prior to a mission.

As from October, not only the Eighth Air Force but also the recently formed Fifteenth Air Force (operating from bases in Italy) would attack targets in Europe. In an attempt to escape the bad weather in the north of Europe a new air force was created, commanded by Doolittle, which would operate out of recently captured bases in the south of Italy. But the prevailing bad weather over the Alps and in the mountains surrounding Foggia meant that this small air force suffered from even more cancellations than the Eighth Air Force.

Bombing by radar would initially be limited to coastal targets, such as Emden, Kiel and Bremen, which were much easier to pick out than targets inland. But accuracy

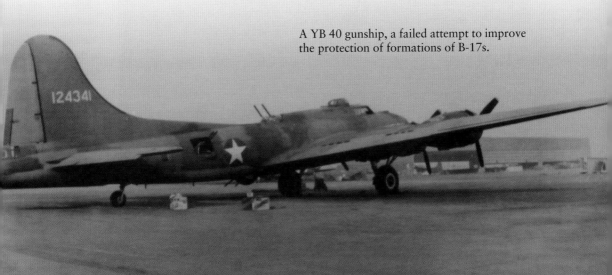

A YB 40 gunship, a failed attempt to improve the protection of formations of B-17s.

was impossible. This was radically contrary to the pre-war doctrine and the requirement to attack only "legitimate" targets and so respect the civil population. Bombing by radar was ultimately the same as the British area bombing the Americans criticized so much. In order to assuage public conscience and opinion, Arnold directed that the term "bombing with navigational devices" be used rather than "blind bombing". But it was yet more evidence that precision bombing was still not enough to win the war.

One advantage of radar was that, as it allowed operations to be flown when there was thick cloud cover, the effectiveness of both flak and German fighters was significantly reduced. The fighters were finding life increasingly more uncomfortable. The American fighters were getting more firepower, better pilots and a longer range, and were operating in huge numbers. Lost aircraft could be replaced by the Germans (in 1944 they still manufactured 40,000 aircraft of all types), but the Americans' aircraft production rate was far superior. In 1944 they built 96,000 aircraft, on top of the number the British and Soviets were producing. But experienced pilots were irreplaceable, and they were being lost at an alarming rate.

1. The best way B-17s could protect themselves was by flying in close formation in order to concentrate defensive fire.

2. A B-17G in flight.

THE H2X RADAR

A high frequency signal was transmitted downwards via an antenna located on the belly of the aircraft in order to scan the terrain below. The return signal created a rough map of the terrain on a cathode ray screen called an oscilloscope. The bomber's radar operator could see an image in which water looked dark, unoccupied land was lighter, and cities shone brightly. Smaller targets such as a factory could not be identified using this primitive system.

Only some aircraft, called pathfinders, were equipped with radar. For radar bombing, when the pathfinders dropped their bombs on the target the other aircraft dropped theirs. Accuracy left a lot to be desired but the qualitative leap was enormous.

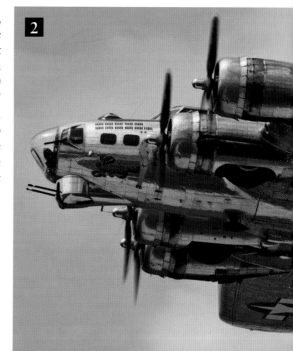

10

Air Supremacy

The Eighth Air Force began to carry out raids escorted by the new long-range fighters, the *Mustang* and the *Thunderbolt*, which could accompany the bombers for the entire mission. By now the force had been dubbed "The Mighty Eighth" and was considered to be an elite unit. The US bombers concentrated on German aircraft factories and production was seriously affected. In response, German aircraft production began to focus on fighter planes and was significantly decentralized. As a result, the number of fighters built grew to an average of 2,500 units a month, although at a cost of reducing the production of other types.

P-38 *LIGHTNING*

The first US aircraft used as a long-range escort fighter (around 900 kilometres) was the P-38 *Lightning*, a twin-engine, twin-boom plane that would be very successful in the Pacific but not so much in Europe. It was very manoeuvrable (although less so than the P-40 it replaced) but at high altitude the performance of its engines dropped off considerably and it fell easy prey to German fighters flown by veterans. At medium and low altitude it was fast, with a maximum speed of 660 km/h.

Its firepower was massive, with one 20mm cannon and four 12.7mm machine guns. Since all its guns were concentrated in the nose, there was no need to set gun convergence at a specific distance which meant the guns' effective range was greater. It could also carry up to 1,000 kg of bombs.

The P-38 began operating as an escort fighter in October 1943, taking advantage of its range of over 2,000 kilometres. Initially it was sent to the Mediterranean theatre although, as from 1944, more would operate over northern Europe.

NEW GERMAN WEAPONS

In order to take on the powerful American four-engine bombers, the Germans began to use two new weapons in some of their aircraft. The 30mm Mk 108 cannon could shoot down a B-17 with an average of three hits, although the gun itself was very heavy. The other new weapon was the 210mm rocket, with a 40 kg explosive warhead. It exploded at a pre-set distance of between 600 and 1,200 metres from the firing point. Some Me 109 versions were fitted with a 30mm cannon, while several Me 110 G twin-engine aircraft were radically transformed to carry four under-wing rockets and forward-facing armament comprising four 20mm and two 30mm cannons. They were heavy and not very manoeuvrable but could deliver devastating firepower.

GERMAN DEFENCES: FLAK

As well as fighters, the *Luftwaffe* had another weapon to bring to bear against bombers; anti-aircraft artillery or flak. Against low flying aircraft the most commonly used anti-aircraft guns were 20mm Flak 38 guns, either single, double or quad-mounted (*Flakvierling*), and 37mm Flak 36 guns.

The main heavy anti-aircraft defence was provided by 88mm guns, of which there were several versions, the most common being the Flak 36. With a practical rate of fire of 15-20 rpm, it fired a 9.4 kg shell with an initial speed of 800 m/s to a maximum height of 10,000 m. The 105mm Flak 38-39 gun fired a 15 kg shell as high as 12,500 m, but there were few deployed. The most powerful gun, the 128mm Flak 40, fired a 26 kg shell to a ceiling of 14,000 m.

They were grouped in batteries, initially of four guns and later of six and even eight guns. Occasionally batteries of twelve guns were formed and, on rare occasions, twenty-four. Guns were initially mounted in open-air emplacements but later they were placed in concrete barbettes to afford a certain degree of protection against attacks on the batteries. In major German cities *flaktürme* were built. These were large towers built of reinforced concrete up to 60 metres tall, equipped with heavy guns on the roof with lighter guns around the outside. They were built in pairs; one tower for the guns and the other for radar and searchlights. They also served as command centres and bomb shelters for the local populace.

The guns were supported by searchlights, the most commonly used being 150cm and 200cm units, and by radar, mainly the Würzburg model, with a range of around 40 km, of which around 4,000 units were built.

The ammunition most commonly used by the 88mm guns were high explosive fragmentation shells, capable of knocking down an aircraft flying within a radius of ten metres from the point of explosion and damaging it within a radius of up to 180 metres. In 1943 they began to use a pre-fragmented shell which produced larger shrapnel pieces. The fuses were set to explode at a certain height, although precision was not good. No really effective proximity fuse ever entered into service.

Flak did not *per se* shoot down a large number of aircraft but it certainly caused a considerable amount of damage to many, leaving them vulnerable to attack by fighters or causing them to crash on the way home or on landing. Flak was also the cause of numerous casualties among the aircrews, for whom its effect on morale was very important, and it helped disorganize close bomber formations and cause them to gain height and so lose accuracy. In 1943 it was estimated that for each aircraft shot down by flak, fighters had shot down 2.9 aircraft, but for each aircraft damaged by fighters, flak had damaged 9.3 aircraft.

The consumption of ammunition was spectacular. In December 1943 it was estimated that 4,000 88mm rounds were needed to knock down each plane. This took its toll on the consumption of resources, to the detriment of other weapons.

The Eighth Air Force calculated that between August 1942 and the end of 1943, fighters had shot down 980 bombers and damaged 1,217, while flak had shot down 239 and damaged 4,691. In the first quarter of 1944 flak shot down 665 bombers and damaged 15,767.

The Allies then concentrated their efforts on attacking synthetic fuel production plants, considerably reducing production by the end of the year. The loss of Romania was the final nail in the coffin and, late in 1944, the *Luftwaffe* no longer had enough fuel to fly even half their aircraft.

But this effort was taking a heavy toll on the Americans. Losses incurred by the Eighth Air Force (and by the Fifteenth, which was already flying raids over the *Reich*) were at the limit of what was sustainable (seventy bombers shot down on 11 January, forty-one on 22 February, and thirty-one on 25 February) but they continued to attack. In March they began their offensive against Berlin, losing sixty-eight bombers on the 6th and thirty-seven two days later. But losses among German pilots were now at alarming levels. Göring ordered that only bombers should be attacked and that engagements with American fighters should be avoided, but this only encouraged the *Mustangs* to be more aggressive.

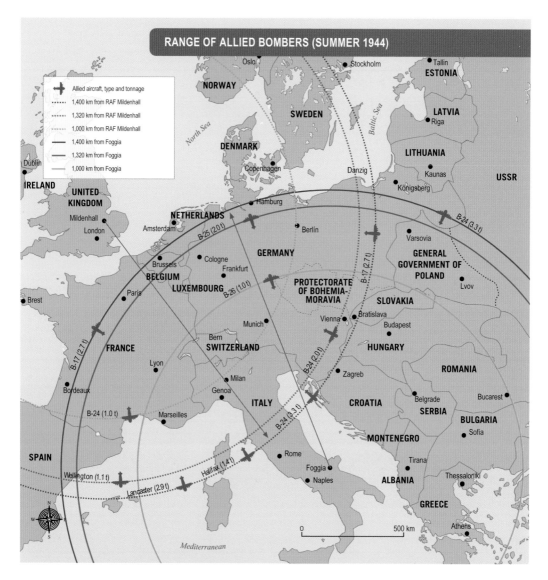

RANGE OF ALLIED BOMBERS (SUMMER 1944)

The British insisted that the Eighth Air Force concentrated on cities so as to simply massacre the civil population in an attempt to show them that resistance was futile and so break their will to go on fighting. *Operation Thunderclap*, a plan to destroy Berlin, was significant in that respect: two thousand aircraft were to attack the German capital and drop 5,000 tons of bombs in an area of less than five square kilometres where 375,000 people lived. If a density of 2,000 tons in 1.5 square kilometres were achieved, 110,000 people would die and about the same number would be injured. The Eighth Air Force were to attack on the first day, followed by the Fifteenth the day after. At nearly every level of the American administration the plan was met with rejection. *"This would be a blot on the history of the Air Force and of the U.S. We should strongly resist being sucked into any such venture... I cannot believe the cause of civilization or world peace would be advanced by killing more women and children."*

By May 1944 the *Luftwaffe* was completely worn-down and overwhelmed in the face of the imminent invasion. *Luftflotte 3* had only 815 aircraft, including 170 single-engine fighters, in all France. The Allies had control of the air and operated as they pleased over French territory, making the daylight movement of German units almost impossible.

On 6 June, D-Day, the gulf between the opposing air forces became all too clear: the *Luftwaffe* flew 100 fighter sorties and 175 bombing raids, compared to a total of 14,600 missions flown by the Allies. Reinforcements began to arrive which increased the number of German aircraft to a thousand, but they had little effect. The Allies took control of the sky in a few days and the ground advance forced the Germans to use increasingly distant airfields. The bombing offensive continued to be devastating and the front was collapsing in the east. In September there were just some 300 German fighters over the Western Front.

The Americans continued to concentrate on fuel production plants and communication systems, but also attacked a number of cities for the somewhat ambiguous purpose of supporting ground troops in the imminent invasion. Munich was attacked in mid-July on the pretext of destroying BMW's factories there, but the familiar lack of accuracy left the city itself seriously damaged. Stuttgart received the same treatment a few days later. The moral shield of the Americans was that the history would judge them more on their intentions than their results, unlike the British.

Thanks to Speer's leadership, the Germans succeeded in restarting synthetic fuel production in a short time, although overall production was gradually declining as a result of the raids. Spaatz responded by intensifying American air raids throughout Germany, although the results obtained were not always worthwhile. Late in August several major raids were flown against Romanian oil plants which caused production to cease. But those facilities were captured by the Russians a few days later anyway.

The *Luftwaffe* concentrated on protecting fuel production and even succeeded in surprising Spaatz. When in mid-September the Eighth Air Force attacked a number of plants on two consecutive days, they were met by a strong concentration of fighters

The powerful *Mustang* with its long range became the ideal escort fighter and a mortal enemy of the *Luftwaffe*.

1

CLARK GABLE

After the death of his wife, the actress Carole Lombard, in an air accident, Hollywood star Clark Gable joined up in the summer of 1942, despite opposition from the studios. Gable enlisted as a machine gunner but Arnold would not allow him to fly combat missions as a gunner. Despite a certain degree of initial scepticism, very soon he earned the respect of his fellow crew members. Afraid of being exhibited as a trophy in the event of being captured he decided not to bail out if his plane was shot down over enemy territory.

In April 1943 Captain Gable filmed a short for Arnold entitled "Combat America", about the air battles of the Eighth Air Force. Sometimes he was able to get away for a weekend break at fellow actor David Niven's cottage. In late October he returned to the United States to edit the movie, which showed the war from a gunner's perspective. Despite containing some of the best footage of air warfare, distribution was limited.

2

and lost 75 aircraft. Towards the end of the month a coordination error caused a group of bombers to find themselves with no fighter escort; within a few minutes the aggressive German fighters shot down 26 aircraft.

Nevertheless, despite the *Luftwaffe's* occasional successes, the situation was irreversible. The constant

1. *Flying Fortresses* lined up at the side of a runway in one of the air bases in the south of England.

2. Another famous flying actor: *Lieutenant Colonel* James Stewart, a B-24 pilot.

bombing of communication systems and fuel plants resulted in German troop movements becoming complicated and costly. Anywhere in the *Reich* could be attacked at any moment; nowhere was safe from the apparently all-powerful Allied air forces. Not only the big four-engine bombers but the ubiquitous twin-engine bombers and fighter-bombers enjoyed nearly total air superiority.

ELECTRONIC WARFARE

Aware of the capabilities of the German Würzburg radar, early in the war the Americans had designed a system called APT-2 *Carpet* to send out a powerful signal to jam that particular radar system. In the autumn of 1943 the first jammers were fitted to a number of aircraft of Groups 96 and 388.

Each device transmitted on a very narrow frequency band so that the bombers in a box could cover the entire spectrum of the Würzburg, between 553 and 566 MHz. Systems were activated when the formation entered a zone swept by anti-aircraft fire and was deactivated once it was clear. On 8 October a formation of 170 B-17s, 42 of which were fitted with *Carpet*, attacked Bremen, losing only 2.4 per cent of its aircraft, a quarter of the losses of another unit that was not equipped with *Carpet*.

FRANCIS GABRESKI

Polish-American Francis Gabreski would become the top American fighter ace in Europe, despite an unpromising start in which he passed his pilot's exams on his last attempt. On the day of the attack on Pearl Harbor he was stationed there but although he succeeded in taking off in a P-40, he was unable to engage the Japanese raiders.

As a captain he was sent to England where he flew in British *Spitfires*, which were far more agile than P-40s. He flew 26 sorties, engaging the enemy on just one occasion. Flying the new *Thunderbolt* he started to fly sorties without much luck. He did not score his first kill until 24 August 1943. He would go on to claim 28 kills in 193 sorties but was shot down over Normandy and saw out the war in a POW camp. He flew in the Korean War as well, where he also became an ace flying jets.

11

Storm Over the *Reich*

In autumn 1944, the priority targets were officially fuel production plants, relegating to second place communication systems and engine factories. In addition to the strategic aim of paralyzing German ground troops by cutting off fuel supplies, there was a moral element in the new directive. The fuel plants were located outside cities, making them ideal targets for precision bombing. Either the target was hit or nothing was. But communication nodes and many factories were another thing entirely as they tended to be in built-up areas. Destroying such targets tended to involve the destruction of purely civil targets and lead to casualties among the population.

There was an attempt to improve the poor accuracy of the bombing (due to the frequent bad weather and the questionable accuracy of the bombsights) by adopting the so-called "drop on the leader" technique, as advocated by LeMay. With this technique only the leader of the formation was fitted with a Norden bombsight and the rest of the formation would drop their bombs when they saw the leader dropped theirs. Overall accuracy improved, but if the leader bombed the wrong target, everyone else did too. It was all or nothing. If the formation had become disorganized, bomb dispersion was inevitable. If the target could not be found there was always some other city to bomb, as in the case of Nüremberg on 8 October or Mannheim on 19 October.

Nevertheless, the raids on German industrial production were taking their toll. The production of synthetic nitrogen and methanol, both required for the manufacture of explosives, had fallen by 63 per cent and 40 per cent respectively, while rubber production was down by 65 per cent. But Germany's capacity to

1. The mechanic's work lacked the glamour of an airman's role, but his work was of vital importance.

2. Formation of P-51s covering bombers.

recover was incredible. In November the Eighth Air Force was met by over 500 fighters in two raids against Bremen. But what could not be recovered was the quality of the German pilots. The bomber formations were growing in size and were protected by larger fighter escorts, which were also very aggressive in the defence of their charges. The huge effort made by the Luftwaffe failed to put a stop to the continuing air offensive.

The front turret of a B-24, with two 12.7mm machine guns.

By the end of 1944 Allied superiority was overwhelming. The Eighth Air Force continued to punish inexperienced pilots mercilessly. On 2 November, seventy pilots were killed in 500 sorties, shooting down a mere seven *Mustangs* in return. The Germans began to concentrate their forces for the *Wehrmacht's* last grand offensive in the Ardennes. They transferred around 1,200 single-engine fighters from other theatres, leaving the air defence of the Eastern Front and the protection of bombers in a precarious state. On 17 December the fighter-bombers flew some 600 sorties against targets in the Allied rearguard but it would be a futile and costly effort.

1 January saw the swansong of the *Luftwaffe*. The Germans launched a mass attack in an attempt to surprise the Allied aviators on the ground and they destroyed 450 aircraft, but at a prohibitive price: they lost 400 aircraft and 237 pilots, 59 of which were irreplaceable squadron leaders. The *Luftwaffe* was dying, and with it Germany's ability to defend the skies over the *Reich*.

Forced belly landing of a P-51.

MUSTANG P-51

The *Mustang* is considered by many to be the best escort fighter aircraft in the war and it remained in service in many air forces until the 1950s (in some cases until the 1960s). With its long range it became the ideal escort fighter for bomber formations both in Europe and in the Pacific.

The original Allison engine imposed serious constraints on what was otherwise an excellent design, but with the adoption of the Rolls-Royce Merlin power unit the performance of the new fighter improved dramatically. Fast, with an excellent rate of climb, manoeuvrable and sturdy, it matched or bettered nearly all its opponents in close combat. It was very well armed with six 12.7mm machine guns and could also fly fighter-bomber missions carrying up to 1,000 kg of bombs and rockets.

Maximum speed was 700 km/h and cruise speed was 580 km/h. The range, with drop tanks, was 2,700 kilometres.

Preparing for the next mission.

American bombers were increasingly more likely to come across new German aircraft, which may have made a difference two years previously but now were a case of too few, too late. The new Me 262 jet fighter (and, to a lesser extent, the Me 163 rocket fighter) were actually a real threat to US bombers, but their impact was irrelevant in the greater scheme of things, since there were so very few of them, their pilots were poorly trained, and their operations were limited by American air superiority and the shortage of fuel.

Despite the priority given to industrial targets, politics gained the upper hand and on 2 February 1945 the Eighth Air Force embarked on a large-scale offensive against Berlin. This ran contrary to the criterion of many commanders who, like Doolittle, considered the offensive to be a pure and simple exercise in terror bombing and, as such, immoral and futile. This offensive was actually *Operation Thunderclap*, conceived the previous year and postponed until now. The British attacked by night and the Americans by day, in a futile attempt to end the war in Europe as soon as possible in order to focus on the Pacific.

Relaxing in one of the Nissen huts.

The campaign of terror was not limited to Berlin. On the 14th it was the turn of Dresden, once again attacked by day and by night. In the last months of the war in Europe the United States succumbed to the logic of terror, seeking destruction for destruction's sake, even though it was useless as a way to hasten victory.

Group of B-17Gs over their target.

A large formation of bombers on their way to the target.

1. Line of B-24s on a British base after a heavy shower.

2. R4 air-to-air missile; a promising concept still in its infancy in 1945.

Next came "Operation Clarion", a coordinated attack by all available Allied air forces against any transportation system targets, by now poorly defended. The operation sought not only material destruction but also the deaths of workers and their families. Late in February, 3,500 bombers and a thousand fighters swept over what was left of Germany, attacking all kinds of targets of opportunity. Once again, although Allied losses were few, the results were not up to expectations. It was clear that the civil population did not want to or was not able to rise up against the Nazi hierarchy to overthrow what was left of the State.

Finally, after three weeks, the US terror bombing campaign ceased early in March. With scarcely two months of the war in Europe remaining, the British continued with their campaign of indiscriminate mass destruction while the Eighth Air Force went back to precision bombing.

Was it Necessary?

While Harris and Bomber Command were demoted by Churchill himself at the end of the war in an absurd attempt at expiation, the commanders of the Eighth Air Force were treated with every honour in the United States. Eaker, Arnold and Spaatz were promoted and had successful careers after the war. Who was right?

The allied bombing campaign over Europe in the Second World War is one of the most controversial subjects of the war. Over two million tons of bombs were dropped on Germany and over sixty cities were destroyed. German industry was seriously damaged and its transport networks destroyed. But industrial production continued almost to the end and only the physical occupation of the territory finally assured victory.

Too few rocket-powered Messerschmitt Me 163 *Komets* entered into service to be effective.

OWN LOSSES

The RAF would lose 22,000 bombers during the long campaign, with the loss of 55,000 airmen. The Americans suffered a similar number of casualties, but lost 18,000 aircraft (an American crew member had more chance of surviving if his aircraft was shot down, plus the Fortresses and Liberators had larger crews). In return they killed over 600,000 civilians. Of the 225,000 American airmen, some 5,000 were diagnosed with "operational fatigue", although the real figure is certainly much higher. Nearly half of those diagnosed suffered permanent psychiatric disorders and would never fly again.

The B-17 received all the acclaim, even though the B-24 carried a larger bombload and there were more of them.

The time when an air campaign alone could achieve a decisive result was still a long way off.

There are two vital questions that always arise when the bombing campaign is discussed: was it justified and did it serve any purpose? The first question is a purely moral one and there is no right answer. At one extreme is the idea that in war it is immoral to cause casualties among the civil population; at the other is the conviction that the ultimate aim is the physical annihilation of the enemy. In the middle is the idea that a limited number of civilian casualties is acceptable, to be considered as collateral damage, insofar as they lead to a faster conclusion of the war, which will ultimately save lives and resources. But how many

lives are acceptable? Where is the limit? That is something which lies in the moral domain, open to endless debate, and on which it is impossible to reach a consensus, since morality is too individual and too subject to change as the circumstances of each society vary. A war will always be a war and it can never be evaluated from a moral standpoint in absolute terms. Were the same scruples applied to the Japanese, not only in the nuclear attacks but also in the fire-bombing of almost defenceless cities? Where do we draw the line between deliberate atrocity and acceptable collateral damage?

The second question is easier to answer. Even with a level of destruction such as that achieved in Hamburg in 1943 the bombers were unable to neutralize the city, but they did however encourage the Germans to diversify production. British area bombing did not only fail to win the war but it may well have helped prolong it, by encouraging the geographic diversification of war industry sites and making it more difficult to identify strategically worthwhile targets.

American "precision" raids against strategic war industry targets and transport

1, 2 and 3. Devastation. German cities were reduced to ashes.

4. The Black Widow heavy night-fighter flew with the Eighth Air Force at the end of the war.

5. The mechanics' shifts were much longer than the airmen's and they received no medals.

Debate. Would the Allies have dared drop the atom bomb on Germany?

networks were probably a little more effective in terms of contributing to the Allied victory, although the degree to which they contributed is a matter of some controversy. There can be no doubt that the lack of fuel and the drastic reduction of mobility inflicted on the *Wehrmacht* by American bombing raids considerably reduced their capacity to fight on the ground. The raids also diverted a vast amount of resources towards the defence of the skies over the *Reich*, preventing them from being used in other theatres. And it should not be forgotten that it bled the *Luftwaffe* dry (without underestimating in any way the steady loss of pilots on the eastern front and, to a lesser extent, the Mediterranean front). In this respect the American campaign was one more highly important element in the combined Allied war effort towards the final victory. In a way, what began as a strategic offensive became a great tactical campaign, which ended up as a strategic failure but contributed to a great many tactical victories.

Destruction. The strategic bombers came to be used on purely tactical missions, with devastating results.

Bibliography

Author's personal interviews with the crew of the *Sally B.*, Duxford, September 2012, and with *Fighter Command* veterans, September 2015.

Armitage, M. (Editor), *Classic RAF Battles: From World War One to the Present*, Brockhampton Press, London, 1995.

Becker, C., *Luftwaffe War Diaries*, Da Capo, New York, 1994.

Bowman, Martin C., *USAAF Handbook 1939-1945*, Sutton, Sparkford, 1997.

Caballero Jurado, C., *Objetivo Berlín*, Biblioteca El Mundo, Madrid, 2009.

Caballero Jurado, C., *Defensa antiaérea alemana*, Tikal, Madrid, 2014.

Dam-Busters, The Amazing Story of Operation Chastise, Aeroplane Special Edition, Kelsey Publishing Group, Cudham, 2013.

Douglas G., *Boeing B-17 Flying Fortress Owners' Workshop Manual*, Odcombe Press LP,

La Vergne, 2011.

Frankland, N., *Bomber Offensive: The Devastation Of Europe*, Random House, New York, 1969.

Freeman, R.A., Airfields of the Eighth: Then and Now (After the Battle), Essex, 1978.

Gibson, G. (VC), *Enemy Coast Ahead – Uncensored*, Crécy Publishing Ltd, Manchester, 2003.

Hansen, R., *Fire and Fury: The Allied Bombing of Germany, 1942-1945*, Penguin, New York, 2009.

Harris, A., *Bomber Offensive*, Pen & Sword Books, Barnsley, 2005.

Hastings, M., *Bomber Command*, Pan Books, London, 2010.

Mason, F., *Battle over Britain*, Profile Publications, London, 1990.

Middlebrook, M., *The Battle of Hamburg: The Firestorm Raid*, Penguin, London, 1984.

Middlebrook, M., *The Nüremberg Raid*, Penguin, London, 1985.

Middlebrook, M., *The Peenemünde Raid*, Penguin, London, 1985.

Middlebrook, M., *The Regensburg-Schweinfurt Mission*, Penguin, London, 1985.

Middlebrook, M., *The Battle for Berlin*, Penguin, London, 1986.

Miller, D., *Eighth Air Force*, Aurum, London, 2007.

Overy, R., *The Bombing War*, Penguin, London, 2014.

Pavelec, S.M., *The Luftwaffe 1933-1945*, Amber Books, London, 2010.

Price, A., *Battle over the Reich*, Chevron Publishing, London, 2005.

Robinson, Anthony, *The Illustrated Encyclopedia of Aviation*, Aerospace Publishing Ltd., London, 1981.

Tubbs, D.B., *Lancaster Bomber*, Ballantine, New York, 1972.

Wood T. & Gunston B., *Hitler's Luftwaffe*, Random House, New York, 1997.

Dresden